CLADDAGH RING STORY
by
CECILY JOYCE

First published by Cecily Joyce in Ireland 1990.
Reprinted 1991.
Printed by Clódóirí Lurgan Teo.

British Library Cataloguing in Publication Data
Joyce, Cecily
Claddagh Ring Story,
1. Claddagh, Galway
1. Title:

ISBN 0 9517058 1 4

CLADDAGH RING STORY
by
CECILY JOYCE

*On this day, 6th December 1989, feast day of
St. Nicholas of Myra, patron of Hope,
I dedicate this little book to honour all who
"Let Love and Friendship Reign".*

ACKNOWLEDGEMENTS

My thanks to all who inspired, helped, guided, encouraged and took a kindly interest in the preparation of this little book, especially my husband Gerald, Frederick, my father, and late mother Marcella, John and Arthur. I would particularly like to acknowledge the originators and organisers of the Galway Quincentennial Festival of the Tribes and Families, 1984, who sparked such widespread interest in Galway's heritage. The debt to all those writers through the centuries who recorded their impressions and experiences, and those of previous ages, especially those whose work I delighted in, and whose names are recorded in the selected bibliography is acknowledged. Special thanks to artists Christopher O'Donoghue, and Paula Joyce; Mac Thomas, Joyce of Joyce Country and the Joyce family Newhall; Professor William Dudgeon Joyce; Professor Etienne Rynne, Tom and Des Kenny, Margaret Murray, Olive Joyce, Peadar O'Dowd, Johnathen Margetts, Professor T. O'Neill, Rev. Canon Forrest, Kevin Joyce, all of Galway; The Hon. Garech Browne; Mary Keegan (née Joyce,); Mr. Donal Begley, Chief Herald of Ireland; the late Dr. Kurt Ticher; Dr. W. O'Sullivan; Douglas Bennett; Donald McPearson; Carlos Zanoni; John De Courcy Ireland; Rev. Fathers Duffner and Aidan Kennedy O.S.A.; Rev. Fr. Wikleann, O.Carm.; Mrs. Anne O'Hara, Rev. Fr. Casey, Maynooth; the National Museum of Ireland, especially John Teehan, Dermot St. John, Raghnall O'Floinn, Felicity Devlin, Valerie Dowling; the Ulster Museum; the National Museum of Wales; the British Museum; the Victoria and Albert Museum; the Administrator, Westminster Cathedral; Rev. Dr. Maurice Dooley, St. Patrick's College, Thurles; the National Gallery of Ireland; the National Library of Ireland; Trinity College Dublin Library; the Ashmolean Museum, Oxford; the Geological Survey Office; An Taisce; Bórd Failte; Clodoiri Lurgan; Peadar Griffin; Miranda Moriarty; CRES; Tony Hurst (photographer) and Tony Colley (designer); Galway County Libraries Executive Librarian Mary Kavangh; The Irish Georgian Society; The Connacht Tribune Ltd., Claire McMyler; Imelda Duffy; The Company of Goldsmiths of Dublin; The Galway Archaelogical and Historical Society.

The Claddagh Ring consists of two hands holding between them or presenting a heart and over the heart is a design like a crown, or a fleur de lis, or coronet. The phrase or posy that usually accompanies the ring is: *Let love and friendship reign*. Among all peoples the union of heart and hands fall under 3 headings:

Sentimental
i.e. Love and friendship, "Here's my hand, and mine with my heart in it." (Shakespeare)

Religious
"He who prays and labours lifts his heart to God with his hand." (St. Bernard)

Patriotic
"The union of hearts, the Union of hands is the flag of our Union forever." It also exemplifies freedom; amongst the Romans a ring was always forbidden to slaves.
A ring is the symbol of authority and of deligated authority when a ring is passed to another.

The Claddagh Ring, because of its tradition, significance and design, today is an internationally recognised token of love, friendship, honour, loyalty, freedom, and hope.

Language of Flowers:

Faithfulness	Blue Violet	(Hands)
Love	Red Rose; Furze (love for all seasons)	(Heart)
Honour and Glory	Laurel	(Crown)
Hope	Hawthorn	
Joy	Wood Sorrel	
Friendship	Ivy	

CLADDAGH RING STORY
by
CECILY JOYCE

Paula Joyce

Note on the author

Cecily Joyce, M.Sc., is a scientist with an interest in family history and the history of art. Inspired by tales of Galway and the Joyce Country, and by the joyful "Galway Quincentennial Festival of the Tribes and Families 1984", she decided to pay tribute to the heritage and spirit of Galway, its people and friends everywhere. The symbolism and relevance of the Claddagh ring seemed to summarise best the spirit of Galway, and the fact that the Claddagh ring story is so bound up with the Joyce Tribe also were good reasons for embarking on the "Claddagh Ring Story".

Richard Joyce of Galway, the earliest known maker of the Claddagh ring was released from captivity as a slave by his Moorish master on the demand of King William III in 1689, he returned to Galway where he worked as a goldsmith three hundred years ago. In 1989, three hundred years later, his story still fascinates and the spirit of his work lives on. His predecessor, Margaret Joyce "Margaret of the Bridges" has an equally romantic connection with the lore of the Claddagh ring, and the story of these two people and the marvellous Claddagh ring and its message is here presented in their honour.

Cecily Joyce (author) 1989.

The Artists

Christopher J. O'Donoghue, Crinkle, Birr, is a talented artist and teacher.

Paula Joyce is a well known painter of flowers. She is a founder member of the Society of Botanical Artists and exhibits her paintings at the Chelsea Flower Show and at the Royal Horticultural Societie's Westminster Shows where she has received numerous awards.

Michael Conneely (Architectural Artist), Frenchville, Galway.

Sir Frederick W. Burton R.H.A. (1816-1900). Born at Corofin, Co. Clare, Burton began his career as a miniature painter. Later, he painted romantic scenes including paintings dealing with life in the West of Ireland. He is buried at Mount Jerome Cemetary, Dublin.

Helen O'Hara painted around Portstewart, Co. Antrim, Belfast, and Lismore, Co. Waterford 1881-1919; died 22nd January 1920. In June 1904 she was elected an honorary member of the Belfast Art Society along with John Lavery, Mildred-Anne Butler and Frank Spenlove-Spenlove.

CLADDAGH RING STORY

List of illustrations:

Paintings

Plates   *Permission of:*

Tables

CONTENTS

OLD CLADDAGH RING

The Old Claddagh Ring, sure it was my grandmother's,
She wore it a lifetime and gave it to me;
All through the long years, she wore it so proudly,
It was made where the Claddagh rolls down to the sea.
What tales it could tell of trials and hardships,
And of grand happy days when the whole world could sing -
So away with your sorrow, it will bring love tomorrow,
Everyone loves it, the Old Claddagh Ring.

With the crown and the crest to remind me of honour,
And clasping the heart that God's blessing would bring,
The circle of gold always kept us contented,
'Twas true love entwined in the Old Claddagh Ring.
As she knelt at her prayers and thought of her dear ones,
Her soft, gentle smile would charm a king;
And on her worn hand as she told me the story,
You could see the bright glint of the Old Claddagh Ring.

It was her gift to me and it made me so happy,
With this on my finger my heart it would sing;
No king on his throne could be half so happy
As I am when I'm wearing my Old Claddagh Ring.
When the angels above call me up to heaven
In the heart of the Claddagh their voices will sing
Saying "Away with your sorrow, you'll be with us tomorrow,
Be sure and bring with you the Old Claddagh Ring"

(Patrick B. Kelly)

THE CLADDAGH RING

The Claddagh ring belongs to a widespread group of finger rings called *Fede* or "Faith rings" which date from Roman times. They are distinguished by having the bezel cut or cast in the form of two clasped hands, symbolising faith, trust, or "plighted troth". *Fede* rings were popular in the Middle Ages throughout Europe, and there are examples from this time in the National Museum of Ireland, Kildare Street, Dublin. The "Claddagh" ring is a particularly distinctive ring; two hands clasp a heart surmounted by a crown. W. Dillon in his publication on "The Claddagh Ring"in the Galway Archaeological Society Journal, Vol. IV, 1905-6, defines the limits over which the ring is worn as "roughly from the Aran Islands on the West, and through all Connemara and Joyce Country to Galway, and then eastward and southward for not more than 12 miles at most. The whole district is the one served by Galway as trade centre. The ring therefore is not a peculiarity of the fisherfolk of the Claddagh village just outside the city of Galway, but became known as the Claddagh ring probably because of the proximity to the city of the large Claddagh fishing community using the ring alone." Huge numbers of Claddagh rings were left with a Mr.Kirwan following the Great Famine 1846/7 which finally had to be consigned to the melting pot as there was nobody to redeem or purchase them, hence the difficulty in obtaining pre-famine examples.

Dillon describes some early rings, one with a mitre-like crown, rings made from coins, an analogous ring from Brittany, a "Munster" ring, also Spanish rings with some similarities. He tells us that the Claddagh ring was the only ring ever made in Ireland worn by Queen Victoria and later by Queen Alexandra and King Edward VII. Their rings were made by Dillons of Galway, established 1750, to whom the Royal Patent was granted and the tradition has been carried on at Dillons to this day. Prince Rainier and Princess Grace of Monaco in 1962 were presented with gifts embodying the Claddagh ring motif set in Connemara marble.

In 1984 when Galway celebrated its Quincentennial as a Mayoral City, the people of Galway presented a specially commissioned 18 carat gold Claddagh ring to President Ronald Reagan.

The earliest examples of Claddagh rings that can be dated are stamped with RI, the mark of Richard Joyce, a goldsmith working in Galway *circa* 1689-1737, of the Joyce Tribe, one of the renowned "Fourteen Tribes of Galway" City. According to Dr. Kurt Ticher in "The Claddagh Ring − A West of Ireland Folklore Custom" (1980) interest in Claddagh rings became dormant after Richard Joyce ended his manufacturing career in the 1730s, and it was revived a generation or more later, probably by George Robinson (Dillon in fact had attributed the earliest ring to Robinson). From then on a number of Galway goldsmiths and jewellers of Galway made Claddagh rings. Their early manufacture was by cuttle-bone mould casting, then the *cire perdue* or "lost wax" process up to the 1840s, when manufacture became commercialised.

SOME MARKS ON CLADDAGH RINGS

From the latter part of the 17th to the early part of the 18th century.

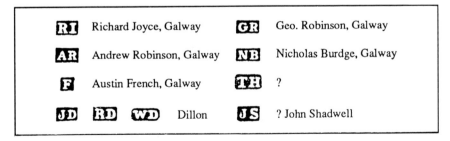

RI	Richard Joyce, Galway	**GR**	Geo. Robinson, Galway
AR	Andrew Robinson, Galway	**NB**	Nicholas Burdge, Galway
F	Austin French, Galway	**TH**	?
JD **RD** **WD**	Dillon	**JS**	? John Shadwell

Dillons of Galway have a fine collection of old Claddagh rings, and of tools used by early goldsmiths. Until relatively recently they used the metal casting with centrifugal force in lost wax process of manufacture.

CLADDAGH RINGS FROM DILLON'S (GALWAY) COLLECTION

(Plate 1)

1.

2.

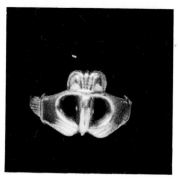

3.

4.

TABLE 1: Claddagh Rings from Dillon's of Galway Collection.

1) George Robinson (GR)1   Assay 17.2 ct. gold
2) George Robinson (GR)2   Assay 16.3 ct. gold
3) Thomas Dillon (TD)   Assay 9.3 ct. gold
4) Nicholas Burdge (NB)   Assay 10.0 ct. gold

Examples of *Fede* and "Claddagh" rings can be seen at various Museums including the National Museum of Ireland, and elsewhere.

TABLE 2: Examples of *Fede* and Claddagh rings in the National Museum of Ireland

Museum Register Number	Description	Maker's Mark
1. 115 (Cat. No.)	Silver. Two Hearts surmounted by crown.	None seen.
2. W241 (Cat. No.)	Gold *Fede* Ring. Two hands holding a heart.	None seen.
3. 113 (Cat. No.)	Silver Claddagh Ring; hoop much broken, roughly repaired.	None seen.
4. 114 (Cat. No.)	Gold Claddagh Ring. Rudimentary crown. Initials PDF engraved inside hoop.	None seen.
5. 1913.18	Gold Claddagh Ring. Rudimentary crown.	T.H.
6. 1922.1	Gold. Child's Claddagh Ring. 18 carat, gold Hallmark.	T.D.
7. 1932.85	Gold Claddagh Ring.	A.R.
8. F1932.86	Gold Claddagh Ring, repaired. Makers mark worn.	J.S.? John Shadwell?
9. F1932.88	Gold Claddagh Ring, 9 carat	T.D.
10. 1954.62	Gold Claddagh Ring. I.P.M. engraved.	F

4

(Plate 2)

1

2

3

4

5

6

7

8

9

10

Photo courtesy of the Photographic Department of the National Museum of Ireland.

5

In the British Museum, London, are examples of two 18th-19th century Claddagh rings – Catalogue No. 1104 with maker's mark R, and Catalogue No. 1105 with maker's mark GR.

The collection of the Victoria and Albert Museum, London, has a ring listed as "English, gold, the bezel in the form of a crowned heart set with diamonds in collets held by two white enamel hands inscribed 'Dudley and Katherine united 26th March 1706'."

Mr. and Mrs. S.C. Hall made a drawing in 1840 of the Claddagh ring with

the following observations (Hall's Ireland 1841): *"They have many peculiar customs: one is worthy of especial note. The wedding ring is a heir-loom in a family. It is regularly transferred by the mother to her daughter first married, and so on to their descendants. These rings are large, of solid gold, and not unfrequently cost from two to three pounds each. The* one we have here copied had evidently seen much service. Some of them are plainer; but the greater number are thus formed."

The Honourable Garech Browne Collection of Claddagh Rings (formally the Dr. Costello, Tuam, Collection) is comprehensive, and includes a Richard Joyce Claddagh ring.

The Honourable Garech Browne "Richard Joyce" Claddagh ring (No. 1).

6

Until the Honourable Garech Browne collection was assayed it was assumed that the Claddagh rings were solid gold. Until 1784 that term meant 22 carat later 18 carat. It was somthing of a shock therefore after assaying, to discover that not only the rings in the Honourable Garech Brown collection, but others examined for fineness, varied from 18 carat at most down to six. At least one ring by Richard Joyce was 18 carat; so were a couple by George Robinson. Dr. Ticher suggests that *"the poor fisherman of the Claddagh made what was for them a great sacrifice to obtain their rings, letting the goldsmiths know how much they could afford to pay. They in turn would have fixed the caratage to bring the ring within the customer's means. In the end, a proud people to whom £3 was a virtual fortune, poverty dictated the fineness of the gold."*

Traditionally, the Claddagh ring was passed from mother to first daughter and worn as a symbol of friendship and as a wedding ring. When it was worn with the heart nearest the finger nail on the right hand, it indicated that the wearer was single and suitors were open to consideration. Placed the same way on the left hand indicated that although the wearer was still single she had an occupied heart. Lastly, when the ring was worn with the crown nearest the finger nail on the left hand, the wearer was married. For the people of the Claddagh the gold ring was often the largest investment they would make.

The Claddagh ring motif has been explained in the phrase or posy "Let love and friendship reign": the hand signifing faith (or plighted throth), the heart signifying love (charity), the crown signifing honour, loyalty, or "hope of future glory".

The Claddagh ring, because of its tradition, significance and design, today is an internationally recognised token of love, friendship, honour, loyalty, freedom and hope.

The town marks of early Galway goldsmiths are the anchor and ship. The anchor is the early Christian symbol of hope, found in the art of the catacombs and on gems. The anchor is also the attribute of St. Nicholas of Myra, patron Saint of Galway. Hope personified, in Gothic Church sculpture, gazes up to heaven and reaches out for a crown, the

7

hope of future glory; an anchor, partly hidden in her robes, derives from St. Paul, who said of hope, "It is like an anchor for our lives . . . it enters in through the veil" (Heb. 6:19); a ship, which may be worn as headgear, is a reminder that early sea journeys were undertaken in a spirit of hopefulness. In flowers, the hope of fruit to come is implicit, hence (from about the 16th century), hope personified may also hold a basket of flowers.

The town marks, the anchor and the ship, chosen by the Galway goldsmiths show that hope was a highly regarded virtue in Galway. The crown in the design of the Claddagh ring may therefore represent hope, as symbolised by the "Crown of Hope" in Gothic Church sculpture. The original Claddagh ring may thus have represented the three theological virtues − Faith, Hope and Charity.

Whatever the symbolism intended by its designer, the Claddagh ring in its workmanship and artistry is a thing of beauty and a joy forever.

TABLE 3: The Honourable Garech Browne Collection
(formally Dr. Costello, Tuam, Collection) of Claddagh Rings
- maker's mark or other identification:-

1) R.I. twice (Richard Joyce) between two sets of initials MRC and possibly HCM (worn)		
2) F	11) SF (1891)	18) None seen
3) GR	12) NB	19) NB. IMM initials
4) AR	13) TM	20) J.S. (1752)
6) AK	14) IJK (Initials)	21) I*C.
7) None seen	15) F	22) M.S. Birmingham (9ct.)
8) T. Meade	16) Birmingham 1870-1 (18 ct)	23) N.B. (1820)
9) ? Sohan, 24 Jan.21. ? Mary Conneely Spiddal	17) GR	24) G.R. (1790)

Note: Ring No. 5 absent, presumed lost.
Ring No. 10 G.R. plain gold band.

The Honourable Garech Browne Collection of Claddagh Rings. *(Plate 3)*

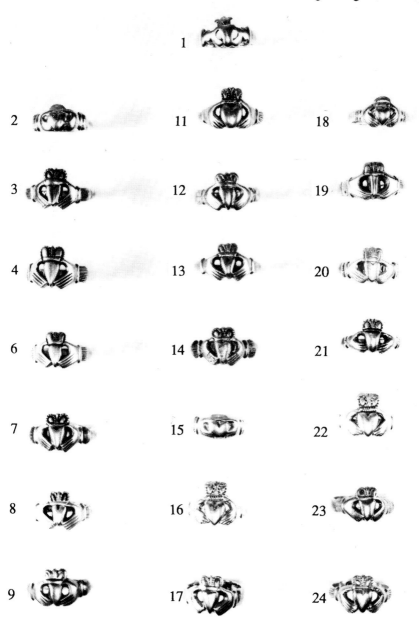

Photograph courtesy of The National Museum of Ireland Photographic Department.

There are two popular versions of the Claddagh ring's origin, both connected with the Joyce family. One story relates it to Margaret Joyce (*fl.* 1596), while the second gives its origin to Richard Joyce the goldsmith whose work dates 1689-1737 approximately, and many examples survive.

The Claddagh Girl - wearing a Claddagh Ring.

C. J. O' Donoghue

THE CLADDAGH RING STORIES

The origin of the Claddagh ring even yet remains a matter for conjecture, but both popular stories of its origins attribute it to the Joyce family of Galway City. The two stories are as follows.

(1) Margaret Joyce married Domingo de Rona, a wealthy Spanish merchant who traded with Galway. They proceeded to Spain, where he died, leaving her a considerable fortune. Returning to Galway she used her fortune to build bridges from Galway to Sligo, and re-married Oliver Og French, Mayor of Galway 1596- 7. She was rewarded for her good works and charity by an eagle who dropped the original *Claddagh ring* into her lap.

(2) Richard Joyce of Galway was captured by Algerian corsairs, sold to a Moorish goldsmith and trained in the craft. In 1689 he was released from slavery as a result of a demand from King William III. The Moor offered him his only daughter in marriage and half his wealth, if he would remain in Algiers, but Joyce declined and returned home. He brought with him the idea of the Claddagh ring. The earliest Claddagh rings to be traced bear his mark and the initial letters of his name, R.I.* (Richard Ioyes).

---

* I and J are interchangeable, they are semi-vowels and can act as either. I at the beginning of a word is a consenant and interchangeable with J — even in English down to the 18th century. U and V are interchangeable for the same reason, as can be observed from inscriptions.

THE STORY OF THE CLADDAGH RING-1

MARGARET JOYCE

Roderick O'Flaherty in "West or H-Iar Connaught" written in AD 1684 tells the story of Margaret Joyce thus:

"Among the founders of pious works, Margaret Joyce Fitz-John, the wife of Alderman Oliver Og French, 1596-7, Mayor, is not to be omitted, who for charity and good commonwealth's sake built severall stone bridges through all Connaught, from Galway to Sligoe. One day as she sat by the work of a bridge, an eagle let fall a golden ring with a precious stone (not known to any lapidary) into her bosom, preserved still by her posterity."

As recounted by Hardiman (1820):

"Heaven was again propitious to another of this family; Margaret Joyes, great grand daughter of the above named William, who was surnamed, Margaret na Drehide, Margaret of the Bridges, from the great number which she built. The story of this singular woman is still current amongst her descendants. They relate she was born of reduced but genteel parents and was first married to Domingo de Rona, a wealthy Spanish merchant, who traded to Galway, where he fell in love with, and married her; and soon after departing for Spain, died there, leaving her mistress of an immense property. Upon his decease, having no issue by him, she married Oliver Oge Ffrench, who was Mayor of Galway in 1596. So far the narrative is probable and consistent, but what follows will try the credulity of the reader. It relates that this lady, during the absence of her second husband, on a voyage, erected most part of the bridges of the Province of Connaught, at her own expense! And that she was one day sitting before the workmen, when an eagle, flying over her head, let fall into her bosom, a gold ring adorned with a brilliant stone, the nature of which no lapidary could ever discover. It was preserved by her descendants, as a most valuable relique in 1661 (the date of the MS from which this account is taken) as a mark supposed to have been sent from Heaven of its approbation of her good works

12

Margaret Joyce meets Don Domingo de Rona.   *C. J. O' Donoghue*

and charity!! This fable though still piously believed, by some of this family, was humorously ridiculed by Latocnaye, an incredulous French traveller, who visited Galway about the end of the last century.''

Chavelier De Latocnaye, a Royalist who fled France after the Revolution was a witty, light-hearted, highly curious young man who walked the length and breadth of Ireland in 1796-7 in the turbulent months before the 1798 Rebellion. Between telling, re-telling, translating, etc. the story as recounted by De Latocnaye would indeed seem incredulous.

"It is said that thirteen families, whose names are still common, laid the city's foundations, and tradition avers that, while a good lady of the name of Joyce watched the masons who built Galway Bridge at her expense, an eagle dropped a chain of gold in her lap, and placed a crown on her head. The gold chain is still preserved by the Joyce family-according to the story told to me."

De Latocnaye also tells us:

"This city had formerly an extensive commerce, but it is much decayed in recent times. Efforts are needed for the encouragement of industry, and it is desirable that some means should be adopted to make beggars work, and prevent lunatics from running about the streets.

A wine merchant gave me, in good faith, an explanation of the decay of commerce. 'Before France knew how to make wine', said he, 'we made it here'.

'What' said I, 'I never heard that you grew grapes at Galway'.

'Oh, we never did,' he replied, 'but in France the wine was simply juice of the grape, and we brought it to Galway to make it drinkable. Unfortunately, the Bordeaux merchants can prepare it now as well as we did, and that has cut the feet from under us'.''

De Latocnaye proceeds to amuse us with the social life of Galway in 1796-7, and its air of merriment and good humour:

"Assemblies where the Galway belles frequenting them could certainly teach their French sisters something in coquetterie. To stay at Galway for three summer months is, for the young folks, a veritable Land of Cockaigne. There are maids who grow old in this city without knowing

Margaret returns to Galway, a widow.

C. J. O' Donoghue.

it, and who continue to shop, dance, and bathe until they have reached the mature age of fifty or more years. Sure I am that nowhere else in any country could they pass the ageing years more agreeably or happily."

It is interesting that we should have the merry atmosphere of Galway described for us by a visitor just before the Rebellion of 1798, as we had the atmosphere described just before another great change in Irish affairs, two hundred years before. Then, Margaret Joyce's husband, Oliver Og Ffrench, Mayor of Galway, wrote the appended letter in 1596 concerning momentious events about to happen in his and Margaret's time. (Appendix).

The story as told in the colourful words of C. S. Otway (1839).

"Margaret, the daughter of John Joyce, who, one day going down to wash her household clothes in the broad transparent stream which runs out of Lough Corrib, and as she stood in the current as did the daughters of Grecian Kings in the time of Ulysses, who should come by but Don Domingo de Rona, a Biscayan merchant of great wealth and note, who had arrived at Galway with a barrack of Benecarlo wine, which was much in demand for doctoring* the claret, the Galway merchants were so famous for concocting.

Now, as fair Margaret beetled away in the stream, and as with ruddy legs and untrammelled toes (as straight and fair as her fingers, not a corn or bunnion on one of them) she trampled the linen, the Don was captivated with the maid; he made love as Spaniards do; produced proofs of his pedigree, and his cash, and in due time they were married, and proceeded to Corunna; but not long after he died (as old cavaliers are apt to do who marry late) and Donna De Rona came home a sparkling and wealthy widow, and by and by her hand was solicited by Oliver Oge Ffrench, one of the heads of that tribe, and in due time they were married, and after the marriage he became mayor and one of the greatest merchants of the city. He traded much to foreign ports, and as it was no shame to smuggle in those days, and as the good town of Galway never was allowed to be lighted by night, in order that smuggling might go on and prosper, so Oliver Oge was often on the sea, showing a good example of enterprise and free trade-exporting wool and importing brandy and wine.

In the meanwhile, the Donna was not idle; she was the greatest improver in the west; she had particularly a passion for building bridges. She might have made as good a pontifex as Pope Joan, and heaven's blessing was on her for her good works; for one day as she was superintending her masons, and eagle came soaring from the ocean, and balancing itself with poised wing just over the dame, it dropped at her feet a ring formed of a single stone, so strange and outlandish in its make and form, but yet so beautiful and so precious that, though the most skilful lapidaries admired it, and would have given any price for it, none could say of what kind it was, or of what country or age was the workmanship; it has been kept in the family since. I wish I could tell the reader which of the Joyces now owns this precious relic. All I can say is, that it is not on the finger of big Jack, or his wife. But indeed the Joyces seem to have been a favoured race; it is a favour that they should be named and known as merry; for he who has 'a merry hath a continual feast'. I assume it to be a favour also that they were under the especial patronage of eagles.''

The story of Margaret Joyce is a romantic and adventurous one and one that obviously has fascinated visitors to Galway since the 1600s. Margaret lived in interesting, colourful and turbulent times. She would have been in Spain during its "Golden Age" and topics and personages still fascinating would have been the order of the day including The Spanish Armada, King Philip II of Spain, Queen Elizabeth I of England, St. Teresa of Avila, El Greco, Cervantes, Shakespeare, Granuale O'Malley, to mention but a few.

---

*It is very well known that the wines of Bordeaux are not adapted to Irish, or indeed, English palates; therefore, the claret that a squire drinks is quite a different thing from the Vin de Bordeaux that a monsieur drinks. The Galway merchants were in the habit of pleasingly doctoring the imported wine to the taste of their customers, hence it was said that they made wine in France, but they made claret in Galway.

"Margaret of the Bridges".

C. J. O'Donoghue

APPENDIX

Letter from Oliver Og French, Mayor of Galway 1596-7
(From the original in the British Museum, Cotton. Lib. Titus B. xiii)
The Mayor of Galway also made the following communication:
'*My most humble duty remembered, may it please your lordship, Hugh Roe O'Donnell, and other the rebells of Tyrconnell, coming of late to this province of Connaght, assembleth with them, Tibbot McWalter Kittagh Bourke, whom he made McWilliam, with all the rebells and renegates of Connaght, wasted, burned and destroyed this last week, almost this whole countie of Galway; wherein, on Saturday last, they sallied Athanrie, burnt the gates thereof, and having entered the same, after continuing there one night, in the morning sallying the castle there, and being withstood, took all the wall-towers, and as manie of the inhabitants as waited them they withhould prisoners, and put to ashes all the rest of the towne, besides the said castell that resisted them, and the bodies of the abbey and churche; and thence afterwards upon Sunday last at twilight, came to our subburbs, and sent a priest and another layman to our gates, then being shut, offering that they would do no harm, if we will relieve them with wine and other necessaries, to which we answered for that night, that we mistrusted, O'Donnell himself was so nigh, and if so was, our auncient custome hath been not to open our gates at night for any affairs, with which the messengers departed. The next morrowe O'Donnell sent a line under his own hand, praying to send him victuals and other necessaries for his money, except powder and ammunition, otherwise he should annoy us the best he could; whome*

17

wee aunsweareth he did pick a quarrell for himself and the rest of his
associates, breaking their allegiance to their natural prince,
destroying townes, contrie and goods, of her maties loyall subjects;
that unless they would revert to goodness, to God, their prince, and
neighbours, we could not afford them no relief. Upon return of which
answer he staid our messanger till he caused divers houses of our
subjects to be fired; and the wind being at east north-east, right
against that side of our town, hindered us much in not discovering the
enemies till the flame was up, and then O'Donnell, Tibott Bourke
McWilliam, McDermoud, and all the chieftaines that were with them,
being in the Abbey- hill, began to retire, and sent some loose shott to
play upon our town, and being confrunted with like loose shott, as the
inimies thronged on this side of the hill, a greate piece of ordinance
was by us discharged, which scattered them, and clustering again
another greater peece was let flie, which utterly daunted them, that
they retired so farr that our loose shott gained the hight of the ridg of
the hill, and saved the houses that were not burnt, and we heare the
rebells had then wounded and killed some vi persons, and that night
camping in the farther part of our ffranchises, sent some bands to fire
the houses that before were rescued from them; but before that
afternoon we discovered them, so that saving one house, lying beyond
the greene, they missed of their purpose, and the day following they
burnt every vilage down to the county of Mayo, and- very well-even to
the poole of Loghcoirbe to leave nothing undesturbed, amongst which
about twenty villages appertaining to us were not pretermitted. Their
speeches, as wee understand, are very blasphemous against us and all
the rest of her majesties constant subjects, threatening they shall
shortly be worse used by the Spaniards, than the poor inhabitants of
Athenry hath been used by them, whom they left mother naked without
anie whitt in the world to live on. And thus, &c. Galway the xixth of
Januarie. your L. most humble at command,

Oliver Oge Ffrench, Maior.

(From the original in the British Museum, *ut supra.*)

Athenry never recovered from the effects of these repeated outrages.

18

Richard Joyce returns to Galway a free man circa 1689.   C. J. O' Donoghue

THE STORY OF THE CLADDAGH RING - 2

RICHARD JOYCE

As recounted by Hardiman (1820):

"Several individuals of this name have long felt grateful to the memory of William III, from the following circumstance, on the accession of that monarch to the throne of England. One of the first acts of his reign was to send an ambassador to Algiers, to demand the immediate release of all the British subjects detained there in slavery, the dey and council, intimidated, reluctantly complied with this demand. Among those released was a young man of the name of Joyes, a native of Galway, who fourteen years before, was captured on his passage to the West Indies, by an Algerine Corsair; on his arrival at Algiers, he was purchased by a wealthy Turk who followed the profession of a goldsmith, and who observing his slave, Joyes, to be tractable and ingenious, instructed him in his trade in which he speedily became an adept. The Moor, as soon as he heard of his release, offered him, in case he should remain, his only daughter in marriage, and with her half his property, but all these, with other tempting and advantageous proposals, Joyes resolutely declined; on his return to Galway he married, and followed the business of a goldsmith with considerable success, and, having acquired a handsome independence, he was enabled to purchase the estate of Rahoon (which lies about two miles west of the town) from Colonel Whaley, one of Cromwell's old officers. Joyes having no son, bequeathed his property to his three daughters, two of whom only were married, one to Andrew Roe French, ancestor of the late Andrew French of Rahoon, to whom, in addition to their own,

19

the unmarried sister left her third; the second daughter was married to the ancestor of the late Martin Lynch, a banker, who, in her right, inherited the remainder of the estate. In gratitude for this act of King William, this family long after solemnised his accession to the throne by bonfires, and his victories in Ireland by exhibiting Orange lilies, on the 1st and 12th July. Some of the Joyes' silver work, stamped with his mark, and the initial letters of his name, are still remaining."

In the 17th and 18th centuries, Corsairs of the North African Barbary Coast (Tunisia, Algeria and Morocco) were powerful enemies to Christian supremacy of the seas. The most famous fast and well-fitted Moslem Corsairs in Atlantic waters were based in Rabat and Sale in Morocco, and known as "Salley Rovers" in these islands. They attacked Christian ships and also coastal towns along the Atlantic coast, and were seen operating as far away as Newfoundland. Their last raid was in 1829.

Today, Essaouira in Morocco is a living memory of the days when Spain, Portugal and England vied with Moroccan swashbucklers for control of the coasts. At the fishing harbour beside the town is the battery left over from those times.

Richard Joyce, on his way to the West Indies around 1675, according to Hardiman (under whatever circumstances), was amongst those captured by Algerian Corsairs and transported to Algeria and slavery until his release *c.* 1689.

Rahoon House still stands and has witnessed much history and changes of ownership through the centuries; today it is the home of the Kelly family. A marriage stone, Joyce and Lynch 1585 remains *in situ* above the right ground floor window of the portico.

There is a reference to Richard Joyce in a Hearth Money Roll for Galway 1724, of the payment of ten shillings Hearth Money (2/6 each for four hearths): Richard Joyce, Shop Street, Papist. (Public Records Office, Belfast.)

In the first quarter of the 18th century members of the "Tribes" donated many silver objects to various convents and churches in Galway, and employed the leading Goldsmiths of Galway, Richard Joyce and

20

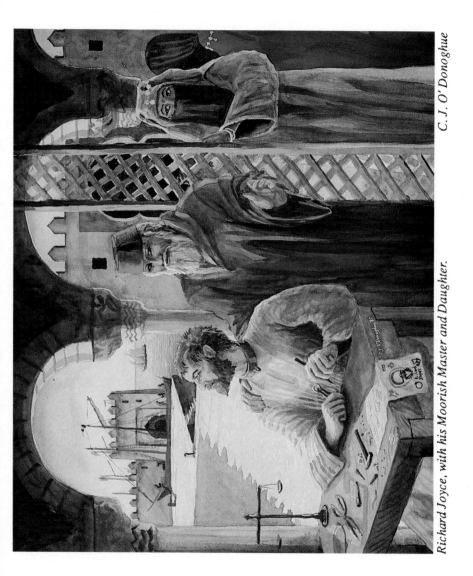

Richard Joyce, with his Moorish Master and Daughter.

C. J. O'Donoghue

Mark Fallon, to produce them. Examples are in public collections, as in the National Museum of Ireland, in Religious Institutions, and in private collections. In his book "Some Irish Altar Plate" (1943), Buckley records many examples of Joyce's ecclesiastical silver-chalices and patens. Dr. Robert Day and Dr. Kurt Ticher describe further works.

Frederick N. Joyce, Joyce Quincentennial Chief at Rahoon House where he lived as a child, once the home of Richard Joyce.

IRISH SILVER

Silver and gold have been highly valued from earliest times. Hope of discovering riches in gold or silver has long lured explorers to chart perilous courses in search of them. They became a measure of wealth and are known as the precious metals. In Ireland we may divide work in the precious metals into three main periods:

(1) Four thousand years ago, gold was crafted into personal and dress ornaments, including collars, bracelets and girdles.

(2) Following the introduction of Christianity to Ireland, from about 500 A.D. to 1500 A.D., work in the precious metals, which were often used in combination with bronze and other metals, was widely practised and the standard of craftsmanship reached a high degree of perfection. The church was then the great patron of the arts in Ireland and much of the metalwork was connected with religious ceremony. Well known pieces such as the Ardagh Chalice and the Tara Brooch (both manufactured about 750 A.D.), the Derrynaflan Chalice (crafted about 800 A.D.) and accompanying paten somewhat earlier, the Cross of Cong probably 1123 A.D., were made during this period.

(3) From 1500 A.D. onwards, silver was the metal most commonly worked, and gold was used mainly for small objects and for gilding. Chalices form the bulk of the articles which have survived from the period 1500 A.D. to 1660 A.D., but after the latter date articles intended for domestic use predominate. The term "Irish Silver" usually refers to pieces manufactured during this era.

From the 12th-14th centuries, the names of some goldsmiths, a term applied also to silversmiths, have been recorded. By the end of the 15th century, a guild of goldsmiths had been formed in Dublin. In 1605, the first reference to hallmarking or stamping of silver occurs, the Corporation of Dublin declared that, due to the use of base silver some goldsmiths were engaged in corrupt practices. To protect the public, each goldsmith was ordered to stamp all wares made by him with his special maker's mark, and to submit the wares for assay in order to establish the proportion of pure silver in the metal. When articles were found to have been made to the required standard they were to be marked with a stamp having the figure of a lion, a harp, and a castle. No pieces bearing this early stamp are known.

In 1637, the Dublin Goldsmiths' Company was established by a charter of King Charles I, and was given powers to control the manufacture and sale of gold and silver wares in Ireland. The Company was obliged to test all gold or silver articles which were made and offered for sale in Ireland, and if the standard of fineness was correct, to stamp them with the Harp Crowned or fineness mark. This mark, in addition to the maker's mark, the date letter, and other marks which were introduced later are together known as hallmarks.

The authority conferred on the Dublin Goldsmiths' Company to control the manufacture and sale of gold and silver wares in Ireland did not initially prevent goldsmiths in Cork, Limerick, Galway, Youghal, Kilkenny and Kinsale from assaying and stamping their own wares. Some articles made by goldsmiths in Waterford, Enniscorthy and Belfast have survived but no distinctive local marks for these centres have been traced.

GALWAY SILVER

Evidence of goldsmiths (encompassing silversmiths) working in Galway exists from early times. The De Burgo O'Malley Chalice of 1494 (in the National Museum of Ireland) was probably made in Galway. Hardiman in 'History of Galway' records Bye-Laws including:

Galway Bye-Law 1500:
"At the request of Andrewe Fallon, on behalf of his daughter Julian Fallon, who is married to Donell Oge O'Vollaghan (O'Nolan) of this towne, goldsmith, and for better relief of said Andrewe, who is old and impotent, the said Donnell made free, on condition of maintaining him."
The names of Walter Davin and Thomas Davin are recorded on a quaint memorial stone dated 1579 in the Franciscan Abbey, Galway, with the goldsmiths' arms and an archaic ship also carved.

Galway Bye-Law 1585 A.D.:
"That the newe statut, made by the goldsmithes, concerning their owne facultie or arte, is commendable, so as they shall observe the same, and mend their former faults."
The Galway mark – an anchor, generally found in a shaped stamp –was first identified by Dr. Robert Day, F.S.A. The first example found, a chalice (procured by Mary Gabriel Skerrett in 1732) marked with an anchor and the initials R.I. is in the Jackson collection now at the Welsh National Museum, Cardiff. A cruet frame of the George I

period with an anchor mark resembling that on the Skerrett chalice but initialled M.F. observed by Dr.. Day while visiting the Rev. Charles Laurence of Laurencetown, Co. Galway, amongst his family plate led to the identification of the marks on the chalice and cruet frame as those of Galway goldsmiths. The Prendergast Chalice of St. Patrick's College, Thurles, clearly marked on cup and foot with the anchor and initials R.I. further led Dr. Day towards the goldsmith Richard Joyce, described in his article "An Old Galway Silversmith".

A mark occurs on a chalice made in the year 1648 for a convent near the Murresk Mountains, RI in a square depression. The chalice in 1921 belonged to the Augustinian Order. The maker could hardly have been Richard Joyce who is mentioned above, and of the "Claddagh" ring story, unless it was ante-dated when made by him, but might very well have been an ancestor of his.

The names of some early Galway goldsmiths are recorded.

Table 4. Names of Galway Goldsmiths recorded 1500-1771

Name of Goldsmith	Date
Donnell O'Vollaghan (O'Nolan)	1500
Walter Davin	1578
Thomas Davin	1578
Nicholas Nolane	1609
R. Ioyes	1648
Richard Joyce	c.1689-1737
?Martin French / Mark Fallon	1696-1730
Bartholomew Fallon	1690-1772
John Shadwell	1757
T. Fitz.-F. Lynch	1771

Richard Joyce (or Ioes) was recorded "Richard Joyce Papist Shop Street, Galway, in 1724. The relationship between Bartholomew Fallon and Mark Fallon is unclear. It is not uncommon for the initials "R.I." and "M.F." to appear on the same article. It has been suggested that Richard Joyce may have taken "M.F." into partnership.

25

From 1784 to 1817 the names of nine goldsmiths are found to have been entered in the books of the Dublin Goldsmiths' Company in pursuance of the provisions of the Act of 1783 which required that all Irish goldsmiths should register their names at the Dublin Assay Office, where all Irish plate, from 1784, ought to have been assayed. Plate made by any Galway goldsmith from 1784 onward would probably be stamped with the Dublin marks. No plate bearing the Galway mark has been found of earlier date than about 1648, and none later than about 1737.

Table 4a: Names of Galway Goldsmiths recorded 1784-1817 in the Books of the Dublin Goldsmiths' Company.

Name of Goldsmith	Date
George Robinson	1784
Austin French	1784
Martin Lain	1784
Laurence Coleman	1784
Francis Dowling	1785
Michael O'Mara	1785
Will. Leathem	1786
James Kelly	1799
Nicholas Burdge W.M.	1817

Austin French and Martin Lain were based in Shop St., Galway; Nicholas Burdge, also a watchmaker, in High St. 1817-1846 at one time worked for Dillons. Joseph Dillon from Barron Strand Street, Waterford, also worked in Galway in 1790.

The Silver Civic Sword of Galway was made in Galway in 1610. The great Mace was made in Dublin a hundred years later and presented to Edward Eyre as Mayor in 1712. Both are displayed in the Bank of Ireland at Eyre Square, Galway.

Richard Joyce purchases Rahoon.

C. J. O' Donoghue

SOME MARKS ON GALWAY PLATE.

The dates in the first column of the table are approximatele and derived from dates inscribed on the articles.

DATE (ABOUT)	MARKS	MAKER'S NAME	ARTICLES
1648	RI	R. Joyes. sen.(?)	De Burgo Chalice
1691	(anchor) RI (anchor)	Richard Joyes	Wine Taster. "1691" engraved on bowl, under initials "P.M."
1700	RI (anchor) RI	Richard Joyes	Foot of Chalice
	(anchor) BF (anchor)	Bartholomew Fallon	Tankard
	EG	Unidentified	Reliquary box
	T.P	Unidentified	Stamped twice on Chalice
1720	I.I	Unidentified	Stamped twice on Galway Chalice dated 1720
1725	RI (anchor) RI	Richard Joyes	The "Prendergast" Chalice
1730	(anchor) MF (anchor)	Mark Fallon	The "Kirwan" cruet frame
1743-45	PI	Unidentified	On wedding-ring, dated 1743, and Freedom box 1745 engraved "Given with freedom of Galway to Captains of East India Fleet. 1745": arms of Galway engraved on lid.

RICHARD JOYCE SILVER

There are examples of the silver work of Richard Joyce in museums, in religious establishments, and in private collections.

TABLE 5: Examples at the National Museum of Ireland

Museum Reg. No.	Year of Manufacture	Example
580-1903	1717	The James Hedye Chalice
39-1929	1717	The Hon. Thomas Burke Chalice
349-1889	1718	F.F.N. Parish Priest of K. & K. Chalice
97-1900	1721	The Geoghegan-Blake Chalice and Paten
21-1926	1729	The Corroll-Lynch Chalice and Paten
60-1932	1737	The Bodkin-Browne Chalice and Paten
349-1933	1720	The Harp Handled Cup
The Kurt Ticher Donation of Irish Silver	*c.* 1720	Pepper Caster (kitchen pepper)

Richard Joyce Chalices at the National Museum, Dublin (Plate 4).

The "James Hedye" Chalice.

National Museum reg. no. 580 - 1903.

Inscribed: "Ora pro Domino Jacobo Hedye Sacerdote qui Instituit hanc calicem fabricari anno Domini 1717."
Noted in the *Journal* R.S.A.I., Vol. 58, page 37.
Deep bowl with everted rim. Eight-facetted globular knop. The foot a tall octagonal pyramidoid with incurved angle and straight base lines, resting on a shallow reeded vertical member. The Crucifixion engraved on three facets of the foot, together with emblems of the Passion. A band of leaf ornament runs around the lower part, and below this the inscription, as above.

The initials of the maker, Richard Joyce of Galway, are stamped once on the bowl and twice on the foot.

Height of chalice, about $8\frac{3}{4}$ ins. Diam. of bowl, about $2\frac{7}{8}$ ins. Width of foot, point to point, about 5 ins.

The "Hon. Thos. Burke" Chalice.

National Museum reg. no. 39 - 1929.

Inscribed: "The gift of the Honble Thoms. Burke for the parishes of Killcooly & Kilrikel Anno Dom. 1717. The Reverent Fathr Morth Donelan Parish Pst."
Sold by auction at Bennett's Saleroom, Dublin, 7th July, 1915.
Deep bowl with everted lip. Octagonal stem with eight-facetted globular knop. The foot an octagonal pyramidoid with incurved angle and straight base lines, resting on a shallow reeded vertical member. The Crucifixion engraved on three facets of the foot. Around the lower part runs a band of leaf ornament, and below it the inscription ,as above. It beas the punched mark "RI" (Richard Joyce).

29

F. F. N. Parish Priest of K. & K.

National Museum reg. no. 349 - 1889. (Buckley 1918 G)

Inscribed: "F.F.N. Parish priest of K and K. Ano Adom 1718.

Also noted in the Journal of R.S.A.I. Vol 58 page 37. Tuam Herald, 1928.

The "Geoghegan-Blake" Chalice.

National Museum reg. no. 97-1900.

Inscribed "Pray for the Souls of Edward Geoghegan and his wife Cisly Blake and Posty 1721".

Deep bowl with everted rim. Facetted baluster stem octagonal in section. The Crucifiction is engraved on one facet; the rest are plain except for the inscription and a narrow border of dogs tooth ornament. A contemporary paten accompanies this chalice. The maker's mark RI (Richard Joyce) is stamped twice on the bowl, twice on the foot, and twice on the paten.

The "Corroll-Lynch" Chalice

Inscribed: "Pray for ye Soules of Edwd Corrol & his wife Mary Corroll alies [sic] Lynch & their Posterity 1729."

In the National Museum, Dublin, reg. no. 21-1926.

Deep bowl, with everted rim. Octagonal stem and eight-facetted knop, engraved with leaf ornament. The foot an octagonal pyramidoid with incurved angel and straight base lines, resting on a shallow fluted vertical member. The Crucifixion is engraved on one facet of the foot, and the inscripition, as above, runs around the lower parts of the other facets. A contemporary paten accompanies this chalice, also a spoon for adding water to the wine before consecration.

Height of chalice, $8\frac{1}{2}$ ins. Diam. of bowl, $3\frac{1}{4}$ ins. Width of foot, $4\frac{3}{8}$ ins. Diam. of paten, $4\frac{1}{4}$ ins.

The maker's mark "RI" (R> Joyes, or Joyce, of Galway) is punched twice on the bowl, twice on the foot, and twice on the paten.

The remains of another inscription are visible on the foot: "PRAY FOR ye Soules of STEPHEN REILLY (?) AND HIS WIFE S..... AND THEIR POSTERITY ANN DOM 17 ..."

The Bodkin - Brown Chalice.

Inscribed: "Pray for ye Souls of Anthoy Bodkin & Catharine Brown Anno Dom 1737."

Deep bowl with everted rim. Octagonal stem with compressed globular knop having eight facets and two engraved bands of conventional ornament. The foot an octagonal pyramidoid with incurved angle and outcurved base lines forming an octafoil outline and resting on a shallow moulded vertical member. The Crucifixion is engraved on one facet of the foot, and an ornamental band

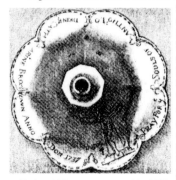

runs around the outer edges of all the eight facets, and above this band the inscription, as above, is engraved. Height of chalice, 8ins. Diam. of bowl, $3\frac{1}{4}$ ins. Width of foot, 5 ins. A contemporary paten accompanied this chalice, and both bear the maker's initials "RI" (Richard Joyce, or Joyes, of Galway).

National Museum reg. no. 60 - 1932.

31

The chalices in the above table are described by Buckley (1943) in "Some Irish Alter Plate", together with the following:

No. 1701c: The John and Agnes Joyce Chalice. The inscription on this chalice indicates that it was made by John Joyce, although this name has not been found recorded amongst goldsmiths. The inscription reads: "Pray for the Soule of John Joyes and his wife Agnes Joyes who made this Challis for the use of the Convent of St. Clare's in Galway 1701".

The fact that a chalice bearing the R.I. mark and 1648 exists together with the above 1701 chalice inscription may indicate successively a family of silversmiths called Joyce in Galway. More research on the circumstances is required.

In Westminster Cathedral, London is a Chalice and Paten described: "An Irish, silver chalice and paten, 22 cms, on moulded octagonal flared foot, engraved with the two Marys and the crucifixion, strawberry knopped stem. Engraved: 'Pray for the souls of Mr. Patrick Fitzgerald and Mrs. Cecily Darsy his wife who caused this chalice to be made for theirs and their posterity. Anno Domini 1719'." The bowl marked by Richard Joyes of Galway, RI, the foot marked MF."

No. 1724b: The Fitz Peter Fitz John Chalice inscribed "Pray for Andw. french fitz Peter and his wife Margt. Joyce fitz John and yr posterity 1724". A contemporary paten accompanies this chalice. On the cup are three punched marks, an anchor and the maker's initials RI (for R. Joyes or Joyce) in an oblong (twice) and on the paten the maker's initials twice.

The weight "1:15" engraved.
Height of chalice 8⅜", Diam. of bowl 3".
Width of foot 4⅜". Diameter of paten 4".

No. 1725a: The Prendergast Chalice (in St. Patrick's College, Thurles where it is still used in the Students' Chapel 1989). This chalice is the one noted by Robert Day FSA. Inscribed: "Pray for Patr. Prenderges and his wife Mary Ann who ordered ys to be made 1725".
Height 9½"; Diameter of bowl 3½"; Width of base 4¼".

No. 1730b: The Edmond Bourke (II) Chalice, in Carmelite Church, Whitefriar Street, Dublin in 1930.

Inscribed: "Pray for Edmond Bourke Parish Priest of Killereran and Famely who Bought me for Ye Honr. of God and Vse of ye Conuent of Ballinsmall Ano Do 1730''.

Bears R.I. and anchor mark.

This chalice in recent years has been at Ballinasmala Friary where Mass is celebrated each year. Ballinasmala Friary was founded by the Prendergasts in the 13th century. The chalice has had an interesting history relating it to the Prendergasts; it was found bricked up in a chimney breast, later given for safekeeping to Prendergast relations of one of the Knock Visionaries, and now used annually at Ballinasmala.

No. 1732c: The Mary Gabriel Skerrett (1) Chalice. Inscribed ''Pray for ye good Intintion of Mary Gabriel Skerrett who procured ys Chalice and Vestment for ye use of ye Infermiry of ye Convt. of St. Clare of Galway 1732''. It bears the maker's mark RI and the anchor mark.

No. 1732a: The Mary Gabriel Skerrett (2) Chalice. Inscribed ''Pray for ye good Intintion of Mary Gabriel Skerrett who procured ys Chalice and a vestiment for ye Use of her Nephew fr. Mark Skerrett 1732''. It bears the maker's mark RI and the anchor mark. Provenance: sold by Patrick Donegan, silversmith, Dame Street, Dublin, to Robert Day FSA Cork about the year 1882. Some ten or twelve years afterwards, the Day Collection of Silver including this chalice was sold in London. Now in the Jackson Collection, at the National Museum of Wales, Cardiff at present.

In July 1989 at an auction at Philips, London a chalice described as follows was offered for sale: "A very rare 18th century Irish Provincial chalice, the plain bowl supported on a faceted stem and cushion knop, the faceted octagonal foot engraved with the Crucifixion and inscribed 'Pray for the soules of Mich. Lynch and his wife Nell Bodkin and their son I. Lynch & Posterty 1721'. Makers mark RI conjoined, struck twice, 19cm high, 8.75 ozs.''

HARP HANDLED CUP.

Two handled cups were originally articles of domestic silver, standard wedding gifts for a father to present. The Richard Joyce Harp Handled Cup of 1720 was probably commissioned for a Donnellan/Colthurst alliance.

Harp Handled Cup by Richard Joyce, 1720, in National Museum of Ireland, Kildare Street, Dublin, with Donnellan/Colthurst Coats of Arms. (Plate 5)

In Ireland today, there are silversmiths who are trained and work using the methods of silversmiths of the sixteenth century. Mr. Donald McPearson has established a group and trains them in the ancient craft of the silversmith at Griffith Avenue, Dublin. Some of the group have now been granted their silversmith's mark by the Dublin Assay Office. Mr. McPearson and Mr. Carlos Zanoni have made an exact copy of the Harp Handled Cup of Richard Joyce at the National Museum of Ireland by the traditional method employing "hand raising". This cup is hallmarked in Dublin in 1989, and is a gesture by these two silversmiths to commemorate the release of Richard Joyce of Galway from slavery in 1689, three hundred years ago — to whom the earliest Claddagh rings are attributed. They also made rings from the "scrap" pieces of silver during the making of the cup as Richard himself must have done three hundred years ago.

Among the Irish Silver on display at the Victoria and Albert Museum, London is a silver tankard with the marks of Mark Fallon and Richard Joyce (Galway Circa 1720) engraved with two crests, a deer's head and a fish.

A most interesting work is described by Dr. Kurt Ticher (1980), a reliquary casket framed in silver, with a copper door, containing part of a skull attributed to St. Ursula. The silver platform is stamped with the maker's mark RI for Richard Joyce Galway *circa* 1723, in square punch three times and once in shaped punch. Inscribed "Pray for sisr Marg' of ye Rosary Joyce who procured ye inclosed Religies of St. Ursalla for ye Domincan Conuent of Nuns Gallway & adorned ym with y casc ye 18 of June 1723". Richard Joyce had many relatives, one of them, probably a niece, Sister Margaret Joyce, who made her profession in 1702 and was Prioress of the Dominican Convent from 1713 to 1716 and again from 1723 to 1726. She embroidered an altar frontal in 1726 and it was she who procured probably from Rome, the relic of St. Ursula for which Richard Joyce made the casket in 1723. The Dominican Convent also has a crucifix by Richard Joyce.

Another interesting example of the work of Galway goldsmiths is the making of Rosaries. There are several "Galway Rosaries" in collections. They range from simple Rosaries of fruit stones to costly ones in ivory, coral, amber and silver. The late Cardinal D'Alton left a "Galway Rosary" to Maynooth College, of amber Ave beads, the Cross and Pater beads are of silver. Many of these Rosaries are similar to Spanish Rosaries.

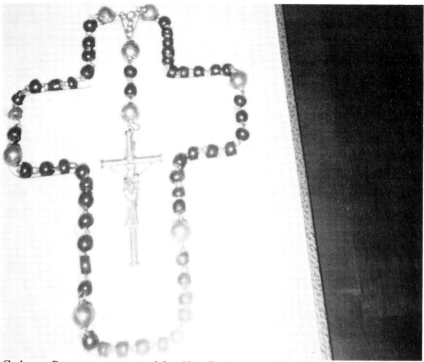

Galway Rosary: presented by His Eminance John Cardinal D'Alton to Maynooth College.

The origin of the Claddagh ring may forever remain shrouded in mystery. Richard Joyce may have got the idea during his years of captivity amongst the Moors, or the idea may have indeed come from the legendary ring said to have been acquired by Margaret Joyce who possibly was an ancestor. The Claddagh ring is similar to the Gimmel ring which during the reign of Elizabeth I and earlier made an end to wooing and to *Fede* rings; the eagle of the legend could indeed have picked a ring up as eagles do, *circa* 1596, and dropped it at Margaret's feet, and both legends of the Claddagh ring may be based on fact. Indeed Fr. Quinn describes a ring made by Thomas Dillon. *"The heart is of stone, a purple red amethyst with two diamonds in the crown"* and suggests that this could be the design possessed by Margaret of the Bridges and handed down to her family.

Donald McPearson and Carlos Zanoni, Silversmiths who today work in the traditional manner, prepare their replica of the Richard Joyce Harp Handled Cup mae in 1989 by the method used by Richard Joyce in 1720.

Donald McPearson, Carlos Zanoni and Dermot St. John.

Hand raising.   *Annealing.*

Wooden hammer on wooden block.   *Planishing.*

38

Replica of Harp Handled Cup,
various components.

Replica of Harp Handled Cup
components assembled.

Replica of Harp Handled Cup
with Coat of Arms of Joyce
of Joyce Country engraved.

Carlos Zanoni and Donald
McPearson, Silversmiths celebrate a
commission successfully completed.

39

THE CLADDAGH

The "Claddagh" is an ancient fishing village sited just outside Galway city, which it may antedate. Hardiman in "The History of the Town and County of the Town of Galway" (1820), describes the Claddagh as "a village situate on the estate of Mr. Whaley". It gets its name from *An Cladach,* meaning a flat, stony shore. Its inhabitants were of Gaelic Irish families and spoke Irish. They lived in a settlement of cobbled streets and small squares flanked by thatched mud-walled houses. Alas, this virtually unique settlement ceased to exist in 1934. The traditional type houses were demolished to make way for more modern concrete replacements.

The Claddagh owed no allegiance to the rulers of Galway but was governed by its own independently elected Mayor or King — the last, Eon Concannon, died in 1934, aged 90. The King was also admiral of Galway Bay and his boat identified by a white sail, instead of the brown or black sails of the rest of the Claddagh fishing fleet.

St. Nicholas, their patron saint, was held in great veneration. The Claddagh people tended to keep to themselves and generally married within the community-thus ensuring the survival of many interesting local customs, including that of the "Claddagh" ring. They employed themselves solely with fishing and activities relating to it, repairing boats, sails, riggings, cordage, nets, etc. When ready, the men departed for their fishing grounds and sometimes remained several days away. When they returned the fish instantly became the property of the women for disposal. The arrival of the shoals of herring, when the whole Claddagh

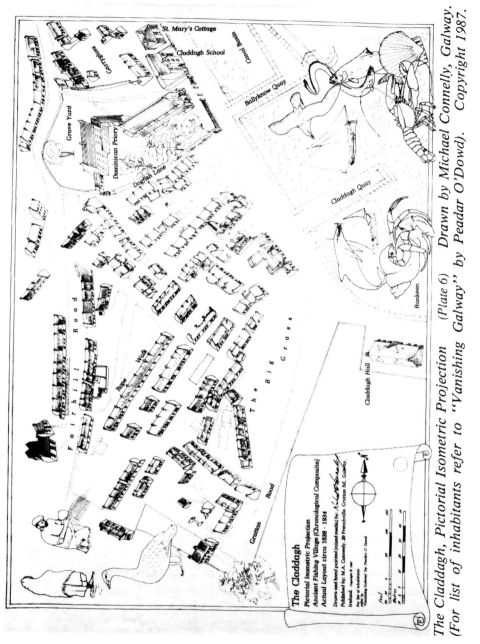

The Claddagh, Pictorial Isometric Projection   (Plate 6)   Drawn by Michael Connelly, Galway.
(For list of inhabitants refer to "Vanishing Galway" by Peadar O'Dowd).   Copyright 1987.

41

fishing fleet gathered and, upon a signal, all sailed out in regular order, was an inconceivably beautiful sight.

The women dressed in a blue mantle, a red body gown, a petticoat of red and a blue or red cotton handkerchief bound around the head. The men wore three flannel vests, under a fourth of white cotton or dimity, trimmed with tape of the same colour, over these a fine blue rug jacket with a standing collar and horn buttons, blue plush breeches never tied or buttoned at the knee, blue worsted stockings, a pair of brogues, a broad trimmed hat neither cocked nor starched, and a red silk handkerchief about the neck on a holyday; at all other times they wore the common jacket and trousers usual with fishermen.

The usual seasons for forming alliances were St. Patrick's Day, the May and September fairs, and Midsummer's Eve. Drinking, dancing and listening to music were the principal amusements. The nativity of St. John the Baptist (24th June) was celebrated by pagentry. On that evening, young and old assembled at the head of the village, their Mayor organised the rank, order and precedence of the procession. They set out, headed by a musical band and marched with continual acclaimations of joy, through the principal streets and suburbs of the town, the young men all dressed in short white jackets with silken sashes, their hats ornamented with ribbons and flowers, and more than 60 or 70 bearing long poles and standards with suitable devices emblematic of their profession. Two of the starters disguised in masks, covered with coloured rags as "Merrymen" with gambols and tricks, made way for the procession. They stopped with loud cheers and salutations opposite the houses of the principal inhabitants from whom they generally received money on the occasion. Returning to the Claddagh, they danced around and sometimes leaped through their bonfires. They brought home part of the fire which they considered sacred. Fire, in fact, did have a special significance for Galway people of old, as did water. Fire, with all its mysteries, played an important part in the religious customs of pagan Ireland, and became christianised as did water as evidenced by the many Holy Wells.

Fire, or bonfires, have pagan and Christian aspects intermingled in such festivities as occurred in Galway during the May Day celebrations, St. John's Night or Bonfire Night, or other celebrations.

Many instances of great longevity occurred. Upon the interment of their dead, they adjourned to a public house in "honour" of the memory of their departed friends. The grief or friendship of each individual was generally estimated by the quantity of liquour which he consumed, or the money which he expended on the occasion.

Arthur Young in *A Tour of Ireland* 1776-1778 gave an account of fishery and potato growing at Galway given to him by Mr. Andrew French of Rahoon, as follows:

"At Galway there is a salmon fishery which lets at £200 a year, and in the bay of Galway they have a considerable herring fishery. There are five or six men to a boat. They fish by shares, dividing into sixty. They have had this fishery time immemorial. The plenty of fish has decreased these fifteen years. All they get is sold into the country, and the demand is so far from being answered, that many cargoes are brought in from the north. The men are far from being industrious in the business, some weeks they do not go out twice. Along the whole bay there is a great quantity of kelp burnt, 3,000 tons are annually exported from Galway. The shore is let with the land against it, and is what the people pay their rent by. They use a great quantity of seaweed, drove in by storms, for manuring land. In November they carry it on, the field being ready marked out in beds for potatoes, and leaving it on them, it rots against the planting season, and gives them great crops. They also do this with fern."

Travellers in Ireland during the decade before the Great Famine of 1845-49 have left us their descriptions of the Claddagh and the people.

John Barrow, in "A Tour Round Ireland: through the sea-coast counties in the Autumn of 1835", notes that the upper part of Galway Bay was literally crowded with fishing vessels, presenting the appearance of a little fleet. The total number of boats employed in the herring fishery alone was 1,500, while the fishing village of Claddagh was inhabited by four or five hundred families. The fishing vessels when the fishing season was over were employed in bringing turf from Connemara to

Galway (from the Claddagh) (*Plate 7*)

Part of the village of Claddagh prior to 1935 when it was demolished.

44

Galway for the supply of the town and the adjacent country; many also transported seaweed for manure from Galway over Lough Corrib for the neighbouring farmers. He also noted that there was no country in the world where fish was more abundant or of finer quality than in all the bays and banks of the west coast of Ireland also that there were then not many countries where so little advantage was taken of such a supply. In his opinion: *"If the fishery were less neglected and more systematically pursued, the harvest would be found equal to a full and cheap supply of this wholesome and nutritive food not only for all Ireland, but also for those Catholic communities on the coasts of France, Spain and Portugal to which the western ports of Ireland afford so easy an access. To Ireland itself, a prompt and energetic prosecution of the fisheries would be one of the greatest blessings that could be bestowed on that unhappy country especially to the poor cottager and the daily labourer, whose families derive a bare existence by feeding on potatoes, moistened perhaps occasionally with a little milk. But the ancient and miserable fishing apparatus of boats and nets the same now as centuries ago together with the dogged habits of the fishermen, are wholly inadequate to meet the demand. The herring and cod fishery alone would furnish an ample supply at one season, and turbot, haddock, hake, plaice, whiting and mackerel at others.*

It is indeed painful to look upon the miserable crafts of the poor fishermen, altogether unfit to brave the stormy Atlantic, that rolls its waves into all the bays and inlets of the Western coast. In fact, the fisheries of Ireland are discouraged by the same cause that pervades and paralyses the whole island want of capital or the want of spirit to employ it. There is, however, another cause that impedes any progress in their improvement the want of regular means of conveyance into the interior, across the mountains or through the passes."

Barrow then proceeds to discuss the advantage of steam communication and looks forward to the building of railroads.

Five years after Barrow's tour, Mr. and Mrs. Hall described the Claddagh visted during their tour of 1840, portraying the people as retaining the customs and habits they have kept unchanged for centuries.

"The inhabitants of the Claddagh are a colony of fishermen and, with their families, number between five and six thousand. Their market place adjoins one of the old gates of the town and is close to the remains of a fortified tower. Here they sell their fish, but it is apart from their own dominion."

The Halls detail their King, laws, rights, customs, the streets, squares and lanes all inhabited by fishermen; the people were in general comfortably clad and their houses neatly furnished. They depict the Claddagh ring also:

In the painting "The Aran Fisherman's Drowned Child" by Frederick William Burton R.H.A., painted in 1841 and bequeathed to the National Gallery of Ireland in 1904, we are presented with a scene set in the interior of a Galway fisherman's cottage, filled with neighbours who have hurried in on hearing of the drowning of the child. The dead child lies across the mother's lap while a woman stands above her, her arms thrown up on high giving vent to a cry, while the unhappy father stands alone staring out of the picture, too shocked for movement or sound, his stance and face expressing the tragedy of the scene. The influence of contemporary painters and of the Old Masters is found in this *genre* painting. The costumes of the women, so exquisitely beautiful and simple, in classically popular colours look as if they belong to a painting by Raphael or Murillo. Details of the kitchen, the core of the Irish home where traditionally a fire was kept burning as a sign of hospitality and of the continuity of life, its contents, the people's clothes and the atmosphere are faithfully recorded. The masts of the boats seen through the open door indicate the presence of Galway Hookers at a pier just outside, thus suggesting that the scene takes place in the Claddagh rather than on the Aran Islands; the fisherman standing alone perhaps is the outsider.

The Aran Fisherman's Drowned Child (1841).   *Sir Frederick W. Burton*

Reproduced by kind permission of the National Gallery of Ireland.

In the Claddagh, many customs still remain such as the religious procession through the streets, especially that on Corpus Christi and the more "secular" one on St. Patrick's Day.

Perhaps, the one most associated with Galway, that of the Blessing of the Bay by the Dominican Fathers, which takes place every August shows that the ordinary folk still value their religious customs.

Blessing the Claddagh Fleet at the beginning of the fishing season (from a sketch by Charles Wymper).

THE CITY OF GALWAY

The origin of the name Galway is a subject of much speculation. One conjecture is that it derives from Gailis-a merchant and ibh-tribe, hence Gailibh-tribes of merchants. Again Galway is said to have been founded in the early centuries when a Celtic King, Breasal,* who was so grieved at the death of his daughter Galvia, who drowned in the river Corrib, that he made a permanent camp on the river bank which later grew into the city so well known today.

The O'Flaherties appear to have had a castle in Galway in early times. Before the Norman invasion in 1169 Galway appears to have been inhabited by a number of families who were principally engaged on the fishing of the lake and bay and in making short voyages along the coast. There names are given as follows: Athy, Branegan, Blundell, Brunt, Burdon, Cale, Calf, Coppinger, Develin or Dilin, Ffarty, Ffrihin, le Fickhill, Kellerie, Kerwick, Lang, Lawless, Moylin, Muneghan, Penrise, Sage, Kancaorach, Valley or Wallin, Verdon, Weider and White.

The Normans however made Galway an important centre of trade, firstly under Walter de Burgo and Richard his son, known as the Red Earl of Ulster. The medieval walled town began to take shape as the merchant families, later to become known as 'The Tribes of Galway' collected taxes (known as murage) on wine, wood, salt, cloth, leather

---

* Breasal's name is associated with the legendary island of Brazil in the West (marked on British Admiralty Maps until 1874) which in turn gave its name to Brazil in South America.

and other goods to build walls around the town. The walls gave security within the city for the merchants to trade. The river Corrib gave access to the north, while the sea allowed foreign trading. On December 15th, 1484, King Richard III granted the charter which raised this most western city to what the late Professor M. D. O'Sullivan called 'The summit of civic independence under a Mayor'. The merchant "Princes" or "Tribes of Galway", held total sway over the town, keeping such valuable positions as the Mayoral office and corporation amongst themselves only. Galway was comparable to many of the European City States of the time, ruled by oligarchies. In the same year, 1484, along with their total civil power the burgesses sought and got Ecclesiastical Independence from the Archbishop of Tuam, when he raised the local church to be the Collegiate Church of St. Nicholas governed by a Warden and Vicars elected by the Corporation. A few months later this was confirmed by a Bull from Pope Innocent VIII. This City State, for this it was in all but name, continued to prosper and develop its trade with France, Spain, etc., in spite of political and religious wars, plagues, famine and disasters which occurred through the centuries.

It has generally been accepted that there were fourteen families who brought Galway to its high state. These fourteen families are known as the fourteen tribes of Galway, namely: Athy, Blake, Bodkin, Browne, D'Arcy, Deane, Ffont, Ffrench, Joyce, Kirwan, Lynch, Martin, Morris and Skerrett.

The families of Galway adopted Coats of Arms which were emblazoned on their stone houses, on the lintels, chimney pieces, tombs, grave slabs, churches etc. and today remnants may be seen.

Many famous visitors to Galway during the sixteenth century have left descriptions of the life in the city, at the time, its opulence, culture, customs, manners, recreations and pastimes, of its pagentry, etc.

From the journal of Sir William Russell, 24th June 1594 – 27th May 1595, we get a picture of Galway seen through the eyes of a visiting viceroy. Like his predecessors, he was officially received with the customary ritual by the mayor and aldermen. They assembled to meet him on his arrival, "The Earls of Kildare, Thomond, and Clanricarde,

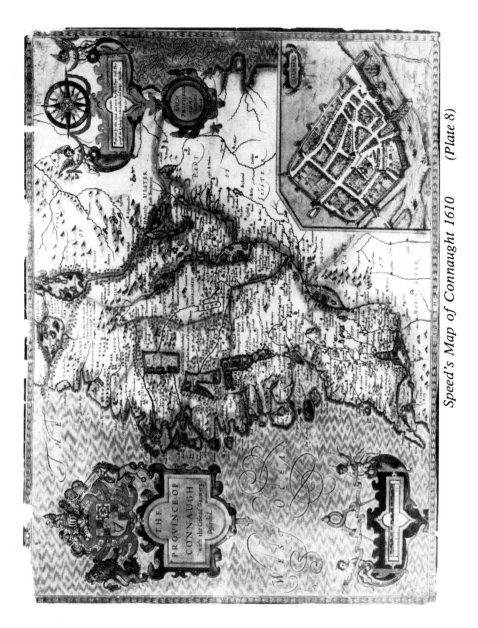

Speed's Map of Connaught 1610   *(Plate 8)*

50

Lords Birmingham, Roche, and Dunkellie, and divers knights and gentleman, who with their retinues resided in the town during his stay. The result was that for some time there was in Galway a succession of festivities – official dinners, private parties, dances and perhaps most interesting, the staging of a masque, that delicate dramatic form only just then becoming popular at the Court in London and at the princely entertainments in the great aristocratic houses in England. The merchants of the city with their ladies met the nobility and landed gentry on equal terms. The burgher aristocracy of Galway were, like their compeers in the Italian municipalities, always counted as of gentle birth. They had, for instance, a right to coat armour which at the time was regarded as the distinctive mark of a gentleman, and they could and did marry on a footing of equality with the neighbouring nobility, Irish and Anglo-Irish. The homes of the merchant aristocracy of Galway were "meet lodgings for Kings and Princes" (MS.1.4.11, Trin. Coll. Dubl.), and the Lynch Castle remains to show how these spacious rooms with their tasteful interior decoration, set off as they were with treasures of plate and tapestry, and lighted with glittering candelabra, must have formed a fitting background for the gay throng who met and mingled with the Lord Deputy and his suite on occasions such as these.

The inauguration of the municipal year at Michaelmas when the Mayor was elected, the colourful religious ceremonies associated with Christmas and Easter, the customary games, bonfires, mummers' performance, the general meetings of the freemen on these occasions and after St. John's Eve-all gave gaiety to the scene and the whole town made merry. The May games, attended by the Mayor and his colleagues resplendent in their robes of office, accompanied by their ladies, were the most interesting of the seasonal pastimes. Houses were decorated with branches of trees and flowers; there was dancing around the Maypole set in a convenient spot in the town, and later bonfires blazed to add to the general gaiety. The games proper, presided over by a Lord and Lady of the May, lasted for three days and included various athletic contests like running, jumping, wrestling, casting of weights, and most spectacular of all, tilting at the ring. On the third day, to wind up the proceedings, the young men were wont to ride out on horseback to Blake's Hill and dine there at a spot between the Hill and the Castle of Barna.

Sir John Harington, famous sixteenth century wit and writer, and one of the best known literary figures of his day, bears striking testimony to the advanced literary tastes in Galway. Harington had translated the "Orlando Furioso" of the Italian poet Arioso (a romantic epic poem about the conflict between Christians and Saracens, 1532 edition) into English in 1591, and in England and abroad his work was much acclaimed. To his amazement, only a few years after his translation appeared, he found it being read with enthusiasm in Galway. *"My Arioso"*, he wrote, *"has been entertained into Gallway before I came. When I got thither, a great lady, a young lady and a fair lady, read herself asleep, nay dead, with a tale of it; the verse, I think, so lively figures her fortune; for as Olimpia was forsaken by the ungrateful Byreno, so had this lady been left by her unkind Calestenes."*

Because their ships went constantly to France and Spain, and further afield, to Flanders, Germany and Italy, the inhabitants of Galway were European-minded. The sons of Galway merchants studied from time to time at Oxford and Cambridge and at some of the great Continental schools, and these young men returned influenced by English and European scholarship and learning. Pilgrimages to the Continent, especially to the shrine of St. James of Campostello, were made and many families had social ties with Spain. The flowering of the Italian Renaissance certainly did not pass unheeded in Galway.

The religion of Galway city remained Roman Catholic, and there was much public devotion (note outdoor altars on 1651 map). Religious orders, i.e. Augustinians, Capuchins, Carmelites, Dominicans, Franciscans, Jesuits, Poor Clares etc. played central roles in city life.

Norman-French was the language used during the early years of development of Galway city. Many inhabitants were well versed in Latin. English later took over as the official language in towns, while Gaelic obviously was employed for communication with those outside the city. Pilgrims and Merchants were familiar with Spanish and French, while those merchants who went to Flanders, Germany and Italy had some familiarity with the languages of these countries.

Regarding the important question of drink, the upper classes patronised wine, though French wine was enjoyed by the fifteenth century, a very definite preference for the vintages of Spain prevailed. The mass of people drank ale, and whiskey, or *aquivitae* as it was generally called in contemporary records, was very popular. Galway was renowned for its hospitality, so much so that in 1518 a law to curb its lavish hospitality was enacted. According to Roderick O'Flaherty's "Iar Connaught' 1684:

'St. Nicholas Bishope of Myra in Licia, worshipped the 6th December on which day Galway men invited to their table such as they would have to keep Christmas next with them'"

Hardiman's Editorial Note 1846 explains: To keep Christmas- *"Galway men" were formerly noted for their hospitality, which they carried to such excess, that the civic authority was often oglibed to interfere, in order to check or regulate it. Thus in A.D. 1518, it was enacted "That no man of this town shall oste or receive into ther housses at Christmas, Easter, nor no feaste elles, any of the Burkes, M'Williams, the Kellies, nor no cepte elles, withoute license of the mayor and councill, on payn to forfeit £5; that neither O ne Mac shall strutte ne swaggere thro' the streets of Galway'.* (Orig. Corporation Book.) After this law, the good people here gradually grew more thrifty.

Several early maps have been made of the city of Galway. In the year 1610, Speed, the celebrated English antiquary visited Galway and his description of the place indicates its then importance. "The principal city of this province", said this accurate writer, "which may worthily be accounted the third in Ireland, is Galway, in Irish Gaillive, built in a manner much like a tower; it is dignified with a Bishop's See" (by this he meant the Wardenship, whose possessions, dignity and extent of jurisdiction equalled those of some Episcopal Sees), "and is much frequented by merchants, by reason whereof, and of the benefit of the road and haven, it is gainful to the inhabitants, through traffick and exchange of rich commodities both by sea and land." To this description was added a map of the town, accurately drawn by himself.

The enthusiasm of the old inhabitants of Galway was boundless when mentioning their native place, their ancient pride and boast, and the source and centre of all their wealth, happiness and connections.

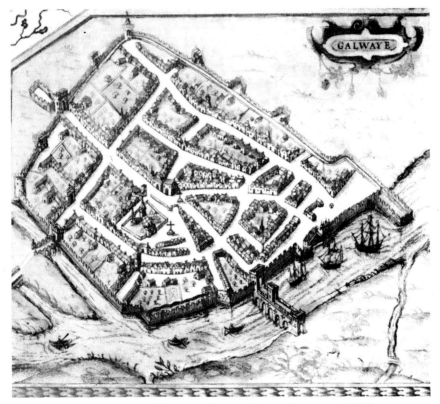

Enlargement of City from Speeds Map of Connaught 1610.

Aly   Blake   Bodkin   Browne   D'Arcy   Deane   Font

Ffrench   Joyce   Kirwan   Lynch   Martin   Skerrett   Morris

THE MAP OF GALWAY CITY 1651

In the year 1651, the Marquis of Clanricarde directed that a map of the town be made, which after the Restoration of King Charles II was finished, blazoned and described by the Rev. Henry Joyce, then Warden, and afterwards elegantly engraved at the expense of the Corporation and dedicated to King Charles II.

The map is composed of nine separate sheets and is six feet six inches broad, and four feet six inches high; it is surrounded by a border, four inches deep. One copy is in the MS Library, Trinity College Dublin; the other was (1820) in the possession of Dominick Geoffry Browne of Castlemagaret, Co. Mayo, and a third was seen in the College of St. Isidore, Rome.

On the right and left margins of the map are contained the armorial bearings, but without names, of twenty-four distinguished families connected with and allied to those of Galway with an inscription (in Latin) at each side. The bottom margin is divided into five compartments, in the first are the armorial bearing of the families of Barrett, Bermingham, Burke, Butler, Crean and Penreice, with this inscription underneath:

'*Conspicuous here the illustrious arms behold,*
Of those whom Galway midst her tribes enroll'd''

In the second compartment, the armorial bearing of the families of Deane, Joyce, Martin and Skerrett with the inscription over "*Antiqua quorumdam Galviae stirpium insignia*'', and the following underneath (Hardiman's translation):-

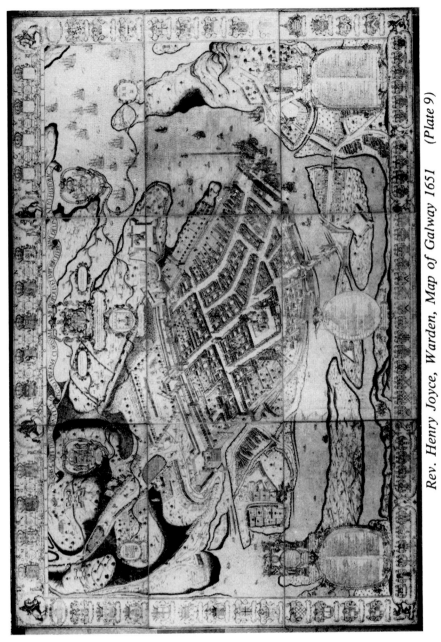

Rev. Henry Joyce, Warden, Map of Galway 1651   (Plate 9)

"The ancient arms of Galway's lords you view
With true obeisance, highest prince, to you. "
In the third, the armorial bearings of the families of Athy, Blake, Bodkin, Browne, D'Arcy, Deane, Ffont, Ffrench, Joyce, Kirwan, Lynch, Martin, Morris, Skerett, with the following verse underneath:
"Rome boasts seven hills, the Nile its sev'n-fold stream
Around the pole sev'n radiant planets gleam;
Galway, Conation Rome, twice equals these;
She boasts twice sev'n illustrious families;
Twice sev'n high tow'rs defend her lofty walls;
And polished marble decks her splendid halls;
Twice sev'n her massive gates, o'er which arise
Twice sev'n strong castles tow'ring to the skies;
Twice sev'n her bridges, thro' whose arches flow
The silv'ry tides, majestically slow;
Her ample Church with twice sev'n altar flames,
And heavenly patron every altar claims;
While twice sev'n convents pious anthems raise
(Sev'n for each sex) to sound Jehovah's praise. "
In the fourth, several armorial bearings of the Lynch family headed with an inscription, and followed by:
"From one proud stock, for ages known to fame
These different branches of the Lynches came. "
In the fifth, the armorial bearings of the families of Fallon, Labarth, Nolan, Quin, Tully and Porte, with:
"Our common rights, these, late enfranchised, prove
And claim a kindred through connubial love. "
In the body of the map are various arms, inscriptions, etc., together with the pictorial representation of Galway. There are two Tables of Reference to the map, the first referring to all matters within the town, the second to all matters outside the walls.

Table of Reference 1 records in detail all the fourteens of edifaces, religious orders, altars, markets etc., mentioned in the poem. Today one can see only traces of the city's former splendour.

57

In the sixteenth century, the Galway merchants employed architects to build them luxurious dwellings, some fourteen of which are depicted on the Pictorial Map of the town. The Browne doorway from the house of Martin Browne, Abbeygate Street, re-erected (1905-06) as an entrance to Eyre Square, and the doorway of the house of Sir Peter French in Market Street are good examples of Renaissance work and show that Galway, at this time, was more under Continental than English influence in art, not surprising when we consider the close contacts of Galway and its inhabitants with the Continent.

The interiors of these houses with their elegant fittings, woodwork, paintings, plate, tapestry, bore testimony to the good taste of the owners and to their liberality as patrons of the contemporary arts and crafts, especially those of the town.

From the description given on the Map, a tolerably accurate idea may be formed of the former opulent state and magnificence of Galway, adorned with superb and highly decorated buildings and surrounded by every requisite for security and defence, while its inhabitants stood conspicuously distinguished for their commercial pursuits, public zeal, and high independence of spirit. Alas, the Cromwellian period lay just ahead.

In Hardiman's time (*circa* 1820), there remained several ancient houses and castles, many in good repair and inhabited. The arms of the different families could be seen in the buildings, and many had subterraneous passages extending beyond the town walls.

Penrice's ancient castle in William Street;
Athy's in Lombard Street;
Blake's mansion-house, at the rere of the Shamble Barrack;
Bodkins (of Carrowbeg) mansion in Back Street;
Bodkins (another branch) opposite the old Augustinian Convent;
Browne's of Castlemagarret mansion house in William Street,
Darcy's mansion house near the Abbey Gate;
Frenches mansion in Market Street;
Frenches of Grenage, in Middle Street;
Joyce's house at the corner of Market Street in Abbeygate Street;

Kirwan's mansion facing the south aisle and tower of the church;
Lynch's Court (of Castlecarra) at the corner of Abbeygate Street;
Martin's of Gregan's dwelling in Market Street;
Martin's of Gort- na-Clevy at the corner of Watergate Street;
Skerrits' ancient residence, which faced the south side of the church.
These ancient houses and castles gradually disappeared so that we
are left today with but one example, Lynch's Castle.

Armorial Bearings of the Tribes of Galway
(Plate 10)

Lynch

Ever Faithful

LYNCH'S CASTLE

Lynch's castle stands as a solitary sentinel to a time when Galway's wealthy merchants lived in such fine medieval buildings, vying with each other in their decoration. The outside of their houses had their Coats of Arms sculptured on stone slabs on the walls and the surroundings of the windows and doorways had stone decorations.

Lynch's castle in style is thoroughly Irish shown by the set off in the dripstone, the tongue shaped corbel, and the interlaced ornament popularly called "Runic".

On Lynch's castle exterior on the Shop Street side are the arms of King Henry VII who reigned from 1485 to 1509, and in a roundel the Coat of Arms of the Lynch family.

On the Abbeygate Street side is a stone roundel containing the Coat of Arms of Garret Fitzgerald, the "Great Earl" of Kildare who freed the town for a time following the Battle of Knockdoe in 1504.

The castle is four storeys high and its layout corresponds very much with that of contemporary merchant houses in the port of Bristol, for instance, in the ground floor was probably a warehouse opening to the street. Above this were the parlours and living rooms, with the bedrooms in the second and third floors, while built out behind was the great hall with a lofty roof of carved timber, and at the end of the hall was situated the kitchen. At first, these houses were the only residences of the burgher aristocracy, but already by the sixteenth century the "Tribe" families had also acquired substantial country homes in the immediate neighbourhood.

The Lynch family provided Galway with 84 Mayors between 1485 and 1654; and Corporation meetinge were held in their castle. This family has endowed a Chapel in the Collegiate Church of St. Nicholas.

Lynch's castle is now a branch of the Allied Irish Bank who have restored and maintain it. It is the oldest Irish building used daily for commercial purposes. Banking in Galway began as early as 1300. From the seventeeth century, Galway merchants issued tokens. In 1802, Walter Joyce and Mark Lynch established a bank in Galway. In 1808, Lynch left and set up a separate and rival bank styled "Mark Lynch, Esq., and Son", whereupon Walter Joyce took into partnership John Appleyard; subsequently, John Joyce and Francis Blake (Cregg) were partners. A bank note of the "Galway Bank" dated 1811 with the names John Joyce and Fran. Blake is displayed at the Heraldic Museum, Dublin.

Lynch's Castle, Galway (1820 view). (Plate 11)

THE CHURCH OF ST. NICHOLAS

In 1320 the building of what was to become the second largest medieval parish church in Ireland, adjoining the old church, commenced. It was dedicated to St. Nicholas of Myra, the patron saint of sailors-this was common in medieval ports depending on trade. Originally, the new church had a cruciform plan, with the nave (congregation area) and the chancel (containing the altar) running in an east-west direction of 152 ft. while the north- south transepts (arms of the cross) extended for 135 ft. It did not retain its original shape for long. A great deal of money (one third of all taxes for a period) was collected and used for its embellishment. This was augmented by generous endowments from the various merchant prince "Tribes" who seemed to have competed with one another to add aisles, chapels, windows, doorways, stone plaques etc. to the original structure so that today we have a very complex building. The church tower dates from about 1500, the large central west window from 1583 and the spire from 1683. The history of the church is linked very closely with the development of the City of Galway, and became a Collegiate Church in 1494, when Galway became a city. The Church has changed hands many times; in 1643 the Catholics returned and were finally dispossessed in 1652.

The Church of St. Nicholas, like the other buildings in Galway, was damaged by the Cromwellians and a particularly regrettable loss is the stained glass in the windows donated at the end of the fifteenth century by James Lynch FitzStephen. This glass, we are told, was considered a most sumptuous and costly ornament. Stained glass work, amongst

Collegiate Church of St. Nicholas, Galway. (Plate 12)

The Cathedral of Our Lady Assumed into Heaven and St. Nicholas (1965)
(Plate 12a)

63

Collegiate Church of St. Nicholas, Galway - some aspects.

(Plate 13)

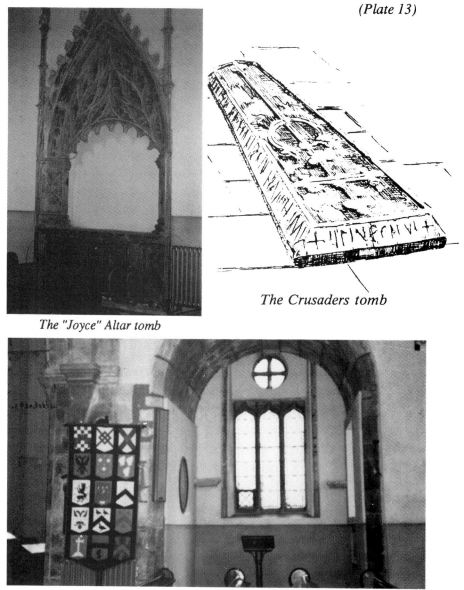

The Crusaders tomb

The "Joyce" Altar tomb

Crusaders Chapel in which is the Crusaders Tomb.
Armorial Bearings of Tribes of Galway on left.

other arts, had reached a very high level of perfection with the Anglo-Normans in the thirteenth century and was introduced by them into some of the towns in Ireland, notably Kilkenny and Dublin. It is probable that the stained glass put in St. Nicholas's Church in the fifteenth century was imported from some other Irish town, possibly Dublin, or from abroad.

There seems little doubt that the interior fittings and the sacred vessels were the products of local craftsmen, the goldsmiths and metal workers of Galway.

Still to be seen inside are medieval water fonts, floor tombstones with trade signs, the Chapel of the Blessed Sacrament (where Columbus himself is said to have heard Mass), the traditionally named leper's gallery and apprentice pillar, a medieval crown and two mitres carved from wood in the Vestry room, the Crusader's tomb, the restored tomb of the Lynch mayor who is said to have hanged his son in 1493, the Joyce Altar Tomb, the stone frame once thought may have contained the legendary painting of "Our Lady of Consolation", now in the Cathedral of Gyor in Hungary, and many other historical artifacts. Today, St. Nicholas Collegiate Church is a place of worship of the Church of Ireland (Anglican Episcopalian).

Our Lady of Consolation

In the churchyard of St. Nicholas's is a monument to three clearly beloved men of Galway. The Claddagh ring is carved over the following inscription on the monument:
"To the memory of
John Skelton Thompson
Francis John Langley Kinkead
Thomas Leopold Roberts
Who all three perished one day
By drowning in Lough Corrib
17th August 1887
Moved by pity for so sad a catastrophe
The citizens of Galway
had this monument erected
They were lovely and pleasant in their lives
And in death they were not divided."

The frank, sincere wording on this touching memorial gives a picture of the kindly nature of the citizens of Galway. The words of the beautiful poem of St. Francis of Assisi "The Song of Brother Sun", Verse 8, come to mind:
"Praise to Thee,
my Lord for Brother Fire
By whom Thou lighest the night,
He is lovely and pleasant,
mighty, and strong."

*Monument with
Claddagh Ring Carving*

The Cathedral of Our Lady Assumed into Heaven and Saint Nicholas a most impressive edifice, was built between October 1957 and August 1965, under the auspices of the late Archbishop Browne of Galway. Over the Altar in the Chapel of St. Nicholas are early seventeeth century carvings, three large panels illustrating the "Coronation of the Virgin", originally from St. Nicholas' Collegiate Church, of most interesting provenance. This is the Roman Catholic Cathedral of Galway (Plate 12a).

GALWAY IN TRADITION AND TODAY

Galway city has an important maritime tradition from its earliest times. Dermod Mór O'Brien, grandson of Teige Aluinn who resided at Tromra in Clare in 1277, received 12 tuns of wine yearly as a tribute from the Merchants of the town in consideration of protecting the harbour and trade from all pirates and privateers by maintaining a suitable maritime force for the purpose. The citizens of Galway always were on friendly terms with the O'Briens. The O'Briens of Tromra in Thomond which was part of the ancient patrimonial estate of the O'Briens of Arran (descendants of Brian Boru) were Sovereign Lords of the Isles of Arran in the bay of Galway and of Tromra in the County of Clare until the sixteenth century when they were expelled by the O'Flaherties of Iar-Connaught.

Granuale O'Malley (*c.* 1530–1603) galleys were a familiar sight passing Galway Bay in pursuance of her adventurous lifestyle.

Galway's important maritime position is underlined by the tradition that Christopher Columbus visited Galway and learned much before finally setting out on his voyage to America in 1492. On that voyage, tradition has it, that he visited Galway and took a Galwayman on board. Recent research suggests that Christopher Columbus set foot in Galway in 1477. The story of St. Brendan the Navigator's much earlier transatlantic voyage was internationally known at the time. St. Brendan had Galway contacts, he founded monasteries at Clonfert in east Galway, on Inchiquin island on Lough Corrib, and perhaps at Ross Hill in Joyce Country etc., and died in 577 at the nunnery which he had founded for his sister at Annaghdown to which diocese St. Nicholas's in 1477 belonged.

Galway today is a prosperous and thriving city, full of energy, a must for tourists, proud of its past and confident of its future. Galway remains the key to the West of Ireland. It opens doors to beautiful and wild scenery of Connemara and Joyce Country and welcomes vistors to the cultural heritage also of Gaelic Ireland. The statue by Albert Power of Padraic O'Conaire in Eyre Square is but a reminder of the heritage which inspired great writers, poets, artists and musicians. Galway celebrated in 1984 the Quincentennial of the year it reached "The Summit of Civic Independence" (1484). During 1984 the "Festival of the Galway Tribes and Families" was initiated; now a notable event on Galway's joyfully eventful social calendar, presided over by its Mayor."

*"In Love and Friendship may Galway's Mayor reign
The Civic Leader of this Joyful City."*

At the Galway Quincentenniel Banquet, July 1984. The Mayor of Galway Cllr. Mary Byrne with Taoiseach Dr. Garret Fitzgerald and other honoured guests of Galway city 1984. (photograph: Connaught Tribune.)

68

Festival of the Tribes Quincentennial Banquet 1984; with the Mayor of Galway, Councillor Mary Byrne are "chiefs" or their representatives.

Front row Representing; Morris, D'Arcy, Galway's Mayor, Joyce, Bodkin. Back row: Athy, Kirwan, Blake, Lynch, Martin, Browne.
(Photograph: Connaught Tribune.)

"Chiefs" elected at Galway Quincentennial Festival of the Tribes and Families 1984:

Athy: Lawrence F. Athy, USA
Blake: James Blake, Blessington
Bodkin: Anne Bodkin-Parker, Letterfrack
Browne: Geoffrey Brown, Galway
D'Arcy: Stephen D'Arcy, Newcastle-under-Lyme, England
(Deane, Ffont: Uncontested)
French: Esther ffrench, Navan
Joyce: Frederick N. Joyce, Clontarf, Dublin
Kirwan: Roderick Kirwan, Rathfarnham, Dublin
Lynch: Patrick V. Lynch, Galway
Martin: Anthony Martyn, Galway
Morris: Hugh Jarlath Morris, Co. Donegal
Skerrett: Martin Skerrett, Corrandulla, Co. Galway.

JOYCE OF JOYCES COUNTRY, WEST GALWAY

O'HART. "IRISH PEDIGREES' (1888)

A very curious pedigree of this family is recorded in the Office of Arms, Dublin.* Some genealogists assert that Joyce and Joy are of Irish origin, and are early branches of the "Mac Sheehy" family; while others assert that they are of Anglo-Norman descent, and were originally called De Jorse. But all admit that they were an ancient, honourable, and nobly descended race; of tall and manly stature; and were allied to the Welsh and British Princes.

Thomas De Jorse, who (according to the History of Galway, &c.) was the first of the name that came to Ireland, sailed from Wales in the reign of King Edward I, immediately after that monarch, A.D. 1282, had defeated the Welsh prince Lewyllen, and added Wales to England. He arrived with his fleet at Thomond, in Ireland, where he married Nora O'Brien, daughter of the then prince of that principality. He afterwards put to sea, steered for West Connaught, and landed in the barony of Tyrawley, in the county of Mayo, where the sept had a temporary stay, and founded the Abbey of Rosserk, on the banks of the river Moy. Thence he re-embarked, and reached Iar Connacht (or the north-western part of the county Galway), where he established a colony and acquired extensive tracts of territory contiguous to Killery Bay, adjacent to the county Mayo; and extending from Cong river to the river Glenbrickeen, near Clifden, in the county Galway, in which some of his posterity now reside. While on his voyage to Iar Connaught, his wife was delivered of a son, whom he named MacMara (or "the son of the sea"), who was subsequently called Edmond. This Edmond

---

*Referred to by James Joyce in *Portrait of the Artist as a Young Man.*

70

(MacMara) Joyce was first married to the daughter of O'Flaherty, prince of Iar Connaught, by whom he acquired the territory comprising the present Parish of Ballinakill, and other districs; from him are descended the Joyces of "Joyces Country", called after their name, now forming the Barony of Ross, the parish of Ballinakill, etc., in the county Galway.

The Joyces were a brave and warlike race, and great commanders of galloglasses, particularly Tioboid na Caislein (Toby or Theobald of the Castles),** who is No. 11 on the list of the chiefs of the Joyce family. This Theobald and the neighbouring chiefs were frequently at war. One of his most remarkable battles was with Tioboid na Luinge (or Toby of the Ships), who is No. 20 on "The Bourkes, lords viscount Mayo" pedigree, which was fought in Partry, on the boundary of the Bourke's territory and Joyce's country, in which the Joyces were victorious, and Theobald Bourke made prisoner.

As the result of that battle, Tioboid na Luinge gave the Joyces a part of his territory, extending from the battlefield (the original boundary; and to this day known as Sraith na Luinge, indicating where Tioboid na Luinge was captured) to Owenbrin. The Joyces were frequently at war with the O'Flahertys, who, during almost the whole of the sixteenth century, strenuously endeavoured to regain the territories which Edmond (MacMara) Joyce received with the daughter of O'Flaherty, as above mentioned.

In 1587 the Clan Joyce, with great valour, opposed Bingham, governor of Connaught, and, assisted by other tribes of the province defeated him at Caislean na Cailighe ("cailleach": Irish, an old woman; Heb. "cheleach" old age), on Lough Mask.

Of the family are the Joyces of Joyce Grove, county Galway; of Oxford, in Mayo; of Woodquay, in the town of Galway; and of Merview, near the town. Other collateral branches of the family settled in Leinster and Munster-a descendant of one of whom was the Irish Judge, Chief Baron Joy. The Joyces of Joyces' Country held their possessions until the middle of the seventeenth century, up to the Cromwellian confiscation; but some of the family are still in possession of extensive property."

Rosserk Abbey.
(Plate 14)

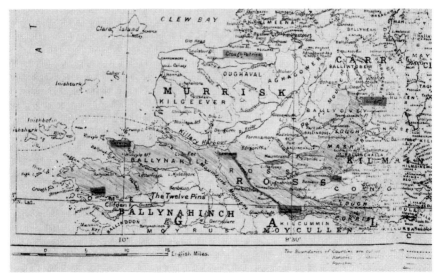

16th century map of Joyce Country and surrounding area   (Plate 14)

72

The Joyces who moved to Galway city and were early included amongst the *"new colonists and septs"* who according to Lynch in his Ms. remarked *"were made famous to the world for their trading faithfully, discharging their credit, good education, charity and hospitality both at home and abroad."*

** Theobald (called Tioboid na Caslein), Chief No. 11, 1570-1600, notable because of all the castles and strongholds he built viz:

> *DOON CASTLE near Clifden.*
>
> *RENVYLE CASTLE which commands the entrance to Killary Bay, (and which stronghold was once unsuccessfully attacked by the famous Grace O'Malley the mother of Tioboid na Luinge above alluded to).*
>
> *CASTLE KIRK, on an island of Lough Corrib commanding the entrance to his territory in that direction.*
>
> *CLONBUR, a stronghold near, on the Eastern boundary of his territory which in Irish is called Duthaig Sheoaigh, and anglicised "Joyces Country", and it is believed:-*
>
> *THE ABBEY OF ROSS HILL adjacent thereto.*

Note: *Renvyle Castle:* Built in the fifteenth century close to the sea at Renvyle. Two walls and two half walls still stand, generally five feet thick, but seven feet thick on the seaward side, and one can still see a part of the typical spiral stone staircase, small windows, and holes where beams once held the floor of the dining hall above. The sleeping quarters were over that. It is now sometimes called Granuaile's Castle. There was in Renvyle a tradition that cannon balls from her ships were embedded on the seaward wall, some were found there by Oliver St. John Gogarty who owned it for some years in the early 20th century.

Castle Kirke, see pages 79-81.

Doon Castle, on the edge of Streamstown Bay. Only slight traces remain, probably as a result of depradations during road building.

Ross Hill Abbey, the original church at Rosshill was built by St. Brendan the Navigator in the site of an ancient circular enclosure near the edge of Lough Mask.

Renvyle Castle.

73

THE HEREDITARY CHIEFS OF THE CLAN JOYCE

The Hereditary Chiefs of Clan Joyce

First Name	*According to O'Hart "Irish Pedigrees" (1888)*	Died
1. Thomas de Jorse		*1317*
2. Edmund (MacMara)		*1346*
3. Walter		*1378*
4. Sir Ulick		*1404*
5. Thomas (2)		*1432*
6. Tioboid (or Theobald)		*1465*
7. Giolla (or Gill)		*1490*
8. Theobald (2)		*1524*
9. Edmond (2)		*1550*
10. Ulick (2)		*1570*
*11. Theobald of the Castles		*1600*
12. Edmond (3)		*1620*
13. Thomas (3)		*1640*
14. Ulick (3)		*1665*
15. Ulick (4)		*1687*
16. Ulick (5)		*1706*
17. Gill (2)		*1731*
18. Theobald (4)		*1751*
19. Giolla (Gill) Dubh		*1774*
20. Theobald (5)		*1790*
21. Gill (4)		*1812*
22. Patrick		*1837*
23. John the Fair (Shane Bán)		*1856*
24. Patrick (2) of Mounterowen House, Leenane		

25. John (2)   1912
26. Patrick (3)   1934
27. John Edward (3), living in Newhall, Co. Clare, in Thomond

John Edward is recognised by The Chief Herald of Ireland as the hereditary chief designate of the Joyce clan or family, called Mac Thomas-son of Thomas who was the first of his name to arrive in Ireland in the 1200s. The Joyce Chiefs' banner is displayed with the banners of the 19 recognised Irish Chiefs of their name in the Museum of the Chief Herald in Kildare Street, Dublin. His title is Mac Thomas Joyce of Joyces Country.

John Edward's father, also John Edward, was second son of Chief John (2) above. His mather was an O'Brien of Thomand; What a coincidence that the present chief lives in the region where the first Thomas Joyce landed, and the heart and hand of Honorah O'Brien, daughter of the then Prince of Thomand was won.

"Marriage of Thomas Joyce and Honora O'Brien."   *C. J. O' Donoghue.*

The Joyces are said to have been a favoured race. In the city of Galway they were known as the Merry Joyces, and *"he who hath a merry heart hath a continual feast"*; but mainly by virtue of being under the patronage of eagles.

The eagle is heraldary, represented with wings:
'displayed', signifies "a man of action, ever more occupied in high and weighty affairs, and one of lofty spirit, ingenious, speedy in apprehension and judicious in matters of ambiguity. "The displayed wings signify protection. The eagle was an ensign of the ancient kings of Persia and Babylon. Marius, 102 B.C. made the eagle alone the ensign at the head of the Roman legions. Since the Romans, many empires and kingdoms have taken the eagle for their ensign, viz, Austria, Prussia, Russia, Poland, France, and the Republic of America. The two-headed eagle signifies a double empire. In Scripture the eagle is a symbol of power.

The eagle is also held to be typical of a noble nature from its strength and innate power and has been very generally preferred in the Continental heraldry as a high device.

The Arms of Connacht are a dimidiated eagle and armed hand.

On the Map of Galway 1651, there are two Coats of Arms for Joyce, the first being amongst the four "Ancient lords of Galway City", having a single eagle; the second, amongst the fourteen 'tribes" of Galway has a double-headed eagle. The Crest with both these Coats of Arms is a demi-wolf rampant, ducally gorged, and the Motto *Mors aut honorabilis vita* - death or a life of honour. The wolf was honoured in ancient Rome. In Galway city on a window moulding still *in situ* the she-wolf symbolism with Romulus and Reymus, is carved.

The older Coat of Arms, the single eagle (Argent), and wolf crest belong to the senior branch of the Joyces and are those of Mac Thomas, Joyce of Joyce Country, Chief of his name. The Coat of Arms with the double headed eagle, and Crest of a "Demi Griffin Sergeant", is registered at the Office of the Chief Herald of Ireland as the branch of the Joyces who moved to Galway city, of Banking fame.

Mors aut
Honorabilis Vita

Joyce of Joyce Country

The Chiefs Banner

The Chief Herald, Mr. Donal Begley with the
Banner of Joyce of Joyce Country.

UNDER THE PATRONAGE OF EAGLES

According to Hardiman (1820), amongst Thomas Joyce's descendants in Galway City, one of the most remarkable was:

"William Joyes, who was married to Agnes Morris, being on his travels from Italy to Greece, he was taken prisoner by the Saracens, and brought to Africa, from whence, after a variety of adventures, and undergoing a captivity of seven years, he escaped to Spain; while here, his exalted virtues were rewarded by heaven, according to the pedigree of this family; in an extraordinary manner; for, as they relate, an eagle flying over his head, pointed out to him a place where he discovered vast treasures; with which returning to Galway, he contributed large sums towards building the walls, church and other public edifices of the town. He died, leaving three sons, James, Henry and Robert, and was interred in the Franciscan Friary."

C. J. O'Donoghue.

78

JOYCES COUNTRY, WEST GALWAY.

The Joyces have for centuries lived in a part of Iar Connaught called
Joyces Country, the Barony of Ross, the parish of Ballinakill etc. It
is a majestic and beautiful place, consisting of brooding mountains,
*"apart and almost terrifying in the massive wisdom of their unnumbered
years, their Gods at rest";* jewel-like lakes, sparkling rivers, holy wells,
desolate spaces, peaceful valleys, rocky ravines with lively cascades,
sea spray and peaceful harbours. Sheep were the gold of the people
of Joyce Country, and herring the silver.

From 1780 to 1810 herring were plentiful around Connemara and
hundreds of fishing ships came to the Killaries, from as far as Scotland.
Then the shoals virtually disappeared until they returned in 1822. The
salt tax made it difficult for the fishermen to sell their fish at a fair
price as they could not afford the salt for preservation and had to sell
immediately. In 1825 the salt tax was abolished, and the fishermen salted
their fish in barrels for their own winter use. Big Ned Joyce, leading
man of the predominant local family, according to Kilroy, was "famous
for going from ship to ship organising a fair price for the whole
community, retaining the old mantle of Chief of his people."

The Western extremity of a finger of Lough Corrib dips into Joyce
Country; here is the fabled island fortress, Caisleán-na-Circe, "Hen's
Castle", or Castle Kirke, which is said to have been built originally
by Roderick O'Connor King of Connaught. It subsequently was the
site of many bloody and brave deeds, changing hands frequently
throughout the centuries. Granuale O'Malley defended it in dramatic

Castle Kirke or Hen's Castle in Lough Corrib (Plate 15)

The Eagle Mountain, Killery. (Plate 15a)

fashion at one period in its history. The Chief of the Joyces, titled "Mac Thomas, Joyce of Joyces Country" had his headquarters there for a considerable period it is recorded, so also at Renvyle and perhaps Lough Mask.

Bounding Joyce Country are Maam Cross, the Maamturk Mountains, Renvyle, Killary, the Partry Mountains, Lough Mask, Lough Corrib and Cong. In the heart of Joyce Country is the beautiful Lough na Fooey, a bright jewel set in a rich ring of majestic mountains. Ashford is famed worldwide for its magical beauty.

Travellers through the centuries have described this inaccessible area of Ireland. Saints of old came to meditate in this region, St. Patrick, St. Brendan the Navigator, St. Feichin of Fore, St. Fursa, etc. Croagh Patrick towers over it watchfully from Co. Mayo.

In the sixteenth century, the Barony of Ross was in the County of Mayo, and later transferred to Galway. Travellers who left details of the wild beauty, and of some of the area's characters, include Blake 1825, Inglis 1834, Barrow 1835, Otway 1839, Mr. and Mrs. Hall 1840 and Thackeray 1842. Big Jack Joyce became a celebrity as a result of travellers' accounts of him. In Inglis's time, he had a house of reception at the head of the Killary:

"Jack Joyce looks upon himself as the greatest man for many a mile around - a sort of king of that country - Joyces Country-as indeed he is. King Dan is a very inferior person to him here." (Daniel O'Connell, the Liberator, who held one of his Monster Meetings in Clifden in 1843). *"No place indeed is more famous for salmon than this same spot and, accordingly, salmon, in all its varieties, was set before me-as much as would have dined a score persons of ordinary dimensions and appetite."*

Barrow (1835) describes Jack's house of industry, spinning wool etc. and his children's education. Today at a hotel in Leenane on the magical Killary fiord one receives a warm welcome, and salmon is still expertly served. An interesting feature of the hotel is the stair balustrade from Chateau Cailly near Rouen, France, incorporating the monogram of Lefebre Caumartin de Cailly, Marquis de Joyeuse.

When Henry Blake came in 1811 to the lands his ancestors had obtained in 1680, as the tall Joyces rowed him down Killary fjord, he felt extremely nervous when the chief of the Joyces expressed surprise that a true Blake could be a Protestant. Nevertheless he was soon reassured of the goodwill of the Joyces. Blake immediately fell in love with the area and its people. He climbed the stone steps of Renvyle Castle and saw a rainbow arching to Inishbofin, saw the moving shadows on the wide expanse of alternating headlands and bays, hills, seas and islands, saw the Twelve Bens magically transformed by a light dusting of snow. He settled with his family in what had been Joyces House, and soon built a larger one with twelve tall chimneys on the site of the present Renvyle Hotel. Here, his wife kept a medicine room, and in the hungary summer weeks before potatoes could be lifted, or during a local potato failure, the Blakes organised supplies of Indian meal and distributed it. (The potato had come to Iar Connaught in 1700). These Blakes were beloved of, and loved the people of the region. After the Famine another Blake family took their place. Oliver St. John Gogarty bought Renvyle early in the twentieth century. Renvyle House was destroyed during the Civil War. It was rebuilt as a hotel, still famous today.

Cecily Joyce and Frederick N. Joyce in 1989 at the grave in Maam valley of John Joyce J.P., the Hereditary Chief of his name, who died on 12th December 1912. Inscription on the gravestone: In Memoriam, Most Sacred Heart of Jesus have mercy on the soul of Margaret Mary Joyce. Died 6th October 1888 aged 49 year, and of her husband John Joyce J.P., Griggins, Died 12th December 1912. The hereditary Chief of his name R.I.P.

Leenane (Plate 16)

Delph Lodge (Plate 16)

83

Dell Allen (née Joyce) (1898 -1986) daughter of Thomas Francis Joyce, was amongst the poets of the Joyce Country. The following poem tells of her feelings for her home place.

Home Again

In the evening hush as the road led homewards,
Over the valley the mist rode high,
Where the hills were grouped in a friendly circle
Shoulder to shoulder against the sky.
By low stone walls and twisting laneways,
Through wooded hollows where trout streams meet,
I crossed the stile by the briar bushes
Over steps worn smooth by passing feet.

Came the murmur of gaelic softly spoken
As the women prayed by the Holy Well,
The scent of hay from the scythe of the mower,
The distant call of the Vesper bell.
The rowlocks creaked as the fishing curraghs
Steered homewards at dusk to the old grey pier -
From byeways clustered with fuchsia blossom
The blackbird's song rang sweet and clear.

'Twas the oil-lamp burning low in its bracket,
Lighting the path to the open door,
The spiral of smoke from a cottage chimney,
The white-washed walls, the old stone floor -
'Twas the little church with its wooded grotto
That nestled close to the dreaming sea,
And, after Mass, 'twas the smiling faces
Of childhood friends that welcomed me.

Swiftly as though the years slipped backwards,
Blotting out memories of laughter and pain.
'Twas a child once more who heard the greeting:
"God bless you, alanna, you're home again!"

In the Maam Valley   *Helen O'Hara (fl. 1881 -1919)*

SELECTED BIBLIOGRAPHY

ALLEN, Dell, *Before the Rains Began,* Recess, Ireland 1977.

BARTLETT, W. H. *The Scenery and Antiquities of Ireland.* London 1840.

BARROW, John, *A Tour Round Ireland, Through the Sea Coast Counties, in the Autumn of 1835,* London 1836.

BEGLEY, Donal, *A Genealogical Record Finder,* Dublin 1987.

BENNETT, Douglas, *Collecting Irish Silver 1637-1900,* London 1984.

BLAKE, Henry, *Letters from the Irish Highlands,* London 1825.

BOURKE, Marie, *Painting in Focus: 'The Aran Fisherman's Drowned Child' by Frederick William Burton,* Ireland 1987.

BURKE'S *Landed Gentry of Ireland.*

BUCKLEY, J. J., *Some Irish Altar Plate,* Dublin 1943.

CHAMBERS, Anne, *Granuaile,* Dublin 1979.

CHAMBERS, Anne, *Chieftain to Knight,* Dublin 1983.

COEN, M., *The Wardenship of Galway,* Galway 1984.

DALTON, O. M., *Catalogue of Finger Rings in the British Museum,* London 1912.

DAY, Robert. *Something about Old Finger Rings,* Belfast Naturelists Field Club. Report and Proceedings. New Series. Vol. I, Part V, pp. 315-318. 1879.

DAY, Robert, 'An Old Galway Silversmith', *Cork Hist. and Arch. Soc. Jrn.* Ser. 2, Vol. X, pp. 230-233, 1904.

DE LATOCNAYE, *A Frenchman's Walk through Ireland 1796-7,* Cork 1798.

DILLON, William, 'The Claddagh Ring', *Galway Arch. Soc. Jn.,* Vol. IV, pp. 11-16, 1905-6.

HALL, Mr. and Mrs. S. C., *Hall's Ireland,* Mr. and Mrs. Hall's Tour of 1840, London 1841.

HARDIMAN, James, *The History of the Town and County of the Town of Galway,* Galway 1820.

HAYWARD, Richard, *The Corrib Country,* Dundalk 1943.

HERALDIC ARTISTS LTD., *The Symbol of Heraldry Explained,* Dublin 1980.

INGLIS, Henry D., *Ireland in 1834,* London 1835.

IRELAND, John De Courcy, *Ireland and the Irish in Maritime History,* Dublin 1986.

JACKSON, Charles J., *English Goldsmiths and their Marks,* London 1921, Revised version 1989.

JOYCE, James, *Portrait of the Artist as a Young Man,* London 1916.

JOYCE, William Dudgeon, *Joyce Country,* Worcester, Ma. USA, 1988.

KENNEDY, Aidan O.S.A.,*The Augustinian Community in Galway in the Penal Times* (from the Housebook, 1724 – 48) Thesis, University College, Dublin.

KILROY, Patricia, *The Story of Connemara,* Dublin 1989.

KNOX, Hubert, *The History of the County Mayo,* Dublin 1908.

MARK, Gordon St. George, *A Silver Chandalier from Galway,* Irish Georgian Society Bulletin. Vol. XXV pp. 19-24, 1982.

NEWMAN, Harold, *An Illustrated Dictionary of Jewellry,* London 1989.

O'HART, John, *Irish Pedigrees,* Dublin 1888.

O'DOWD, Peadar, *Old and New Galway,* Galway 1985.

O'DOWD, Peadar, *Vanishing Galway,* Galway 1987.

O'CEARBHAILL, D., *Galway Town and Gown,* Galway 1984.

O'FLAHERTY, Roderick, *Chorographical Description of West or H-Iar Connaught 1684* (ed. James Hardiman 1846), Dublin 1846.

O'NEILL, Thomas P., *The Tribes and other Galway Families,* Galway 1984.

O'NEILL, Timothy, *Merchants and Mariners in Medieval Ireland,* Dublin 1986.

O'SULLIVAN, M. D., *Old Galway,* Cambridge 1942.

OTWAY, Caesar, *A Tour in Connaught,* Dublin 1839.

PACK, Greta, *Jewelry and Enameling,* London/Canada 1941.

QUINN, Rev. George "The Claddagh Ring". *The Mantel. Vol. XII No. 1* pages 9-12. Spring 1970.

RYNNE, Etienne, *Tourist Trail of Old Galway,* Galway 1977.

SEMPLE, Maurice, *Where The River Corrib Flows,* Galway 1988.

SMITH, Ernest A., *Working in Precious Metals,* London 1933.

THACKERAY, William Makepeace, *The Irish Sketch Book 1812,* London 1843.

TEEHAN, John, *Irish Silver,* A Guide to the Exhibition, Dublin 1979.

TENISON, C. M., *The Private Bankers of Ireland,* Cork Hist. and Art, Soc. Jrn. Vol.II, 1893 p.205.

TICHER, Kurt, Galway Silver in a Dominican Convent, *The Antique Dealer and Collectors Guide,* pp. 71-74 Oct. 1977.

TICHER, Kurt, The Silver in the St. Clare's Monastery, Galway, *Galway Arch. and Hist. Soc. Jn.,* pp. 62-77, Vol. 37, 1979-80.

TICHER, Kurt, The Claddagh Ring. A West of Ireland Folklore Custom. *Antique Dealers and Collectors Guide,* p. 42, Aug. 1980.

VILLIERS-TUTHILL, Kathleen, *Beyond The Twelve Bens,* Galway 1986.

YOUNG, Arthur, *A Tour in Ireland (1776-1778),* London 1780.

YOUNGS, Susan, *The Work of Angels,* London 1989.

WILDE, Sir William R., *Lough Corrib, its shores and islands,* Dublin 1872.

Calendar of State Papers Ireland 1596-1597, Dublin 1893.

Galway Corporation Manuscripts.

Journal of the Galway Archaeological and Historical Society.